I am very familiar with the author, Barbara Arnett. I know of her dedication, preparation, and depth of insight into God's "salvationistic" program. I have had the opportunity to hear several of her presentations on various topics of inspiration. I am sure that her writing will be of inestimable value to anyone who might read after her.

—REV. DR. ISAIAH SCIPIO

The message in *Wisdom, Worship, and the World* is based on Barbara Arnett's personal experiences and work in the local church as a Bible teacher, intercessor, and international Evangelist. I highly recommend this book to anyone who desires to increase in revelation knowledge, wisdom, and worship, and impact the world for Jesus Christ.

—PASTOR THOMAS DALECKE

WISDOM, WORSHIP,
AND THE WORLD

CREATION
HOUSE
A STRANG COMPANY

BARBARA J. ARNETT

WISDOM, WORSHIP, AND THE WORLD by Barbara J. Arnett
Published by Creation House
A Strang Company
600 Rinehart Road
Lake Mary, Florida 32746
www.creationhouse.com

All Scripture quotations are from the King James Version of the Bible.

Cover design by Ededron J. Hernandez

Library of Congress Control Number: 2005930411
International Standard Book Number: 1-59185-894-1

06 07 08 09 — 987654321
Printed in the United States of America

LOVINGLY DEDICATED TO GERT

1923–2004

Gertrude was an extraordinary woman of wisdom, faith, and character. She faced many hardships as she was growing up on a Chippewa Indian Reservation. Overcoming many obstacles in life, Gert was a survivor. She embraced many different people from various walks of life who were a part of her extended family. Her ministry, reaching out to help those who were in need, was a ministry of love.

Contents

Part III: The World

Part I:
Wisdom Now

CHAPTER 1

Think About This for a Moment

NO SANE HUMAN being ever wants to make the same mistakes over and over again, getting the same results over and over again. Many people have great ideas and engage in purposeful activity, but without godly wisdom, ideas and activity may give birth to temporary success. However, the Scripture states in 3 John 2, "Beloved, I wish above all things that thou mayest prosper and be in health, even as thy soul prospereth." God's desire is for us to be successful in all things. His wish is for us to be healthy, to be successful in our souls, and successful in the economic arena." This is God's prayer for you and me. He wants us successful as long as we live on the earth, and for all eternity. These three areas—successful health, success of the soul, and economic success—encompass all that a person could desire in life. If all of the categories were listed under each of these three major headings, nothing would be lacking of the things that one could hope for and desire for himself and his family.

It is very important to God how a person conducts his or her affairs in each of these areas. Health success affords the opportunity to live a long, fulfilled life, and enjoy your success. Soul prosperity guarantees eternal life. In terms of economic success, money should leave an indelible mark that says one has made the world a better place in which to live. Wisdom is the key to success in these areas.

It is available to all—and it is affordable.

My purpose is to help you understand that God has given wisdom so that all can achieve success in this life and in that which is to come. Some people choose to be foolish, however, and others choose to pervert wisdom. There are some individuals who are truly seeking wisdom, and who desire to tap into the Infinite Wisdom Source. These are the ones to whom this book is addressed. You already realize that you need wisdom in your home, wisdom in business. You know that wisdom is necessary for healthy relationships, in your marriage, your family, and in your life. Getting wisdom, knowledge, and understanding is easy, but you must be committed to getting it. You must be consistent, persistent, tenacious, but not ostentatious in your pursuit. If you are the person who expends time, energy, and money to do something that will either directly or indirectly benefit mankind, God wants you to be successful in your efforts and endeavors every time.

Begin your pursuit of wisdom with this confession: I am receiving wisdom, knowledge, and understanding from the Infinite Source of all wisdom. I am committed to this pursuit, and I will be consistent, persistent, and tenacious. I will not be ostentatious as I acquire wisdom, but I will help others tap into the wisdom source. My heart is open to receive godly wisdom for my health, wisdom for my family, wisdom in my relationships, wisdom in business, and wisdom for spiritual development and success. Lord, I thank you, for this opportunity to exercise wisdom daily.

Think of your God-given ideas—creative thoughts, concepts, insight, and purposeful activity—as seeds. Begin to consider everything you do—work, play, prayer, relating to others, money spent, errands, and study—as seeds that you sow into the world for the purpose of making it a better place. Even your time of relaxation, rest, and sleep is a seed sown to keep yourself in good health. When you are in good health, you can help someone else. Some seeds will fail to grow and develop. They do not have to, but without wisdom at every level and stage of development, a seed will fail to reach full maturity. Without wisdom's daily nourishment and water supply, a seed cannot sustain life no matter how much you love it, or how much it will benefit others.

Let me explain with a parable. Parables, by the way, conceal wisdom secrets that God reveals in due season. In Matthew 13, we find the parable of the sower who went out to sow his seed. Some of his seed fell by the wayside and the birds *devoured* them. Some of the seed fell on stony places where there was not enough earth for them to grow, and the sun *scorched* them. They *withered away* because they had no roots. Some seed fell among thorns and the thorns *choked* them. This sower was very careless with his seed. He should have carefully researched the ground and tested the soil before planting. He should not have allowed the seed to fall in just any place. The devoured, the scorched, and the choked had potential and ability to mature and become successful. Some of the seed represents ideas, which had great potential from conception, but were allowed to fall by the wayside. The sower did not realize their potential. Once this happened, they were left with no one to care for them. Then, strangers picked them up and devoured them. They never had an opportunity to grow and develop. Some represent endeavors which were not sown in a nourishing environment. He had no knowledge of the kind of environment his concept needed for adequate development. Because the environment was inadequate, these seeds of greatness were scorched and their potential withered away. The sower made no provision to protect his creative thoughts, which were a different kind of seed. Then, deception came in and choked these seeds to death. The seed represents all kinds of spiritual, family and personal endeavors, affairs of government and society, business ventures, and entrepreneurships.

If God wants us to prosper and be successful, and I know that He does, then our efforts should never be devoured, scorched, or choked. The sower lacked wisdom regarding his seed's potential, their individuality, and how to nurture them until they had become huge fruit-bearing trees. Nevertheless, the unwise sower continued to sow his seed, and as he did, we see how the mercy of God intervened in his life. The last group of seeds sown by the sower were *wise seeds*. Because the sower was unwise, God placed wisdom in the seeds. Through miraculous intervention they fell on good ground and brought an abundant return, some one hundred fold, some sixty, some thirty, and some a thousand times more than they were. This parable demonstrates that the seeds were not to blame for their sad demise. They were at the mercy of the sower. The fact that all of the seed had potential for greatness is seen in the last group. The sower is without a doubt the reason why the first three groups of seeds failed. He depended on his luck for their success. He had no plan of action for his seed: no goals, objectives, strategies, or outcomes. He just let them fall haphazardly. The result was a disaster for the first three groups. The sower was responsible for their lack of success.

Once, I went into a foreign country to take afghans, sheets, pillowcases, clothes, and Beanie Babies to a children's outpatient surgical hospital. The hospital had notified me that they would close on Wednesday at 1 p.m. for the holidays. Another hospital that I had planned to visit was going to close a part of its facility on Tuesday and Wednesday. So I rescheduled the visits for both hospitals on Thursday, forgetting that the children's hospital closed at 1 p.m. on Wednesday. When I arrived at the children's hospital, and found that it was closed, I was very disappointed that I could not deliver the Christmas gifts to the children. We left for the other hospital. While there, I told the missions director what had happened and asked if he had any suggestions regarding how I could get the items to the children's hospital, as I would be back in the U.S. when the hospital reopened after the holidays. As we were talking, there was a couple sitting near us in the cafeteria. The wife was a patient at the hospital. She said she knew of an all-girls orphanage that was really in need, and could use the gifts. The missions director thought that giving the items to the girls orphanage was a good idea. I also felt that it was a "God idea." The man's wife was being discharged from the hospital later that day. They would personally deliver the gifts to the children, and give the orphanage directors our pictures and address. To make a long story short, we handed the children's gifts over to this couple. We anticipated hearing from the couple, the orphanage director, and the children, within a short period of time after returning to the U.S. To this day, we have heard not a word from the couple or the orphanage. What happened to my seed? It was devoured. It was a God idea to give the items to the orphanage. It was a bad idea to give them to the couple. There was a moment, during this transaction when I sensed "wisdom's warning." It came as a flash of insight regarding the man's character. Through a statement he made, and the manner in which he made the statement, I sensed the warning. What I said to myself, at that moment, in response to his statement was, *this woman who is being treated for terminal cancer, who is fighting for her life, would certainly not be plotting with her husband to do something that could bring adversity into her life and his.* She had initiated the conversation about the girl's orphanage.

Giving gifts to the orphanage represented the seed. The couple represented the devourer. Lets follow the stages of this seed's development:

- Stage 1. Idea to take gifts to a children's hospital for the less fortunate.

- Stage 2. Purchase the gifts.

- Stage 3. Pack the items and take them safely into the country that had been identified with the need.

- Stage 4. Dates confused about delivery.

- Stage 5. An alternative means of delivery to the children's hospital is discussed.

- Stage 6. Strangers who happen to be listening to our conversation suggest an alternative to the children's hospital. (This is where the devourer subtly enters the picture.)

- Stage 7. The children's gifts are handed over to the devourer. The point at which the life of a God idea has come to an end. The orphanage idea was acceptable, because needy children would have gifts for Christmas, and subsequent items would be given to the children's hospital at a later date.

Here is a word of wisdom: Deliver your own goods!

CHAPTER 2

Forget That Mess
and Get Some Wisdom

ISDOM. YOU WERE born with it. It is lying dormant within you, waiting for any occasion to arise and demonstrate its splendor and magnificence. The Bible said of Moses in Hebrews 11:23 when he was an infant, "his parents saw that he was a proper child." The Bible also says in 2 Samuel 12:24 that "the Lord loved Solomon" the infant son of Bathsheba and David. In Proverbs 20:11 we read, "Even a child is known by his doings, whether his work be pure, and whether it be right." What happened to this wisdom? I believe that as we mature the cares of the world cause us to not only lose our "childlike faith," but the issues of life suppress our awareness of the God-given wisdom we received supernaturally from birth. If this wisdom had been consistently nurtured from childhood into adulthood, it would have increased a thousandfold in the mature adult. It should never have been lost. God has to restore, refresh, and replenish the wisdom He already placed in our hearts and minds even before the womb. The Lord spoke to Jeremiah saying, "before you came forth out of the womb, I sanctified thee, and ordained thee a prophet unto all the nations of the earth." (See Jeremiah 1:5.) No prophet whom God has chosen and ordained to go and speak to the nations on His behalf is without wisdom. Therefore, at one time, you had wisdom and authority to speak to the nations of the earth for God, and become an international capitalist for Christ. Where did they go?

Godly wisdom is in the earth. It came into the world through Jesus Christ, and it is still in the earth today through the Holy Spirit, who will abide forever. This means that there is always an opportunity for everyone to redeem the wisdom that was lost during some stage of development. You can redeem and recover all, and get more than you received before the womb. You do not have to make another foolish decision or mistake. Instead, get the wisdom back that you received during your "before the womb" ordination.

You must redeem your God-given wisdom. And when you have secured it, gather knowledge and understanding around you like a warm blanket in winter. These three should be your constant companions and most cherished friends. Proverbs 7:4 tells us to, "say unto wisdom, you are my sister; and call understanding our close kinswoman." In my opinion, the greatest commandment ever spoken by God is this one, "Get wisdom: and with all thy getting get understanding" (Prov. 4:7). We should never speak a word, make a decision, or take any action without first seeking God for His infinite wisdom. For the person who is tired of making mistakes, godly wisdom is what you need.

Life's experiences and the environment teach many things, but wisdom is the greatest teacher. Before any endeavor is undertaken, wisdom calls—before a mistake is made, wisdom calls—in the midst of a mistake, wisdom calls—when one behaves wisely, wisdom calls to give an increase in wisdom. Are you listening? Can you hear the call?

WHO'S IN CONTROL—THE SPIRIT OR THE SOUL?

Some of the greatest challenges in my life have made me acutely aware of the "soul nature's" desire to do everything based on emotions and self will. The doctrines of men develop out of emotions and selfishness, or "soulishness." The wisdom of man always arises out of his soul. However, the spirit of a man always moves by the wisdom of God, which is God's will and desire. (You can find definitions for *soul* and *spirit* in *Strong's Concordance* and *Webster's Dictionary.*) The desires of the will must be placed under the authority of the will of God before the fullness of the Spirit of God in wisdom, knowledge, and understanding can be experienced.

The spirit of man is a powerful force. The natural man contends with the spirit for control over decision making and action taking through head knowledge and natural thinking. In Proverbs 20:27 the Bible says, "The spirit of man is the candle of the Lord." Just as the Spirit of God searches and thoroughly examines the profound mysteries and secret things of God, the spirit of man was created to search and intensely examine "the deep things of God" also. The natural man (or the soul nature) cannot perceive or discern the mysteries of God because God will not reveal spiritual matters in a natural way. Spiritual things are not organized, or presented in a format that will appease the soul. The natural mind wants to understand revealed spiritual truths and godly wisdom through emotions, imaginations, statistical research, guesswork, and feelings. However, spiritual matters are perceived, understood, and discerned by *faith*, which is spiritual substance. A person must believe that God exists, and that He rewards those who diligently seek Him through faith. Without this faith no one can please God. As a matter of fact, "Without faith it is impossible to please [God]." (See 1 Corinthians 2:10, 11, 14; Hebrews 11:6.) The wisdom seeker exercises self-control and discipline, training the spirit and renewing the mind through study of the Bible and prayer to receive God's wisdom and respond appropriately to it.

THE PRINCIPAL THING

Solomon, the son of King David, is the greatest expert on wisdom the world has ever known. He declared the Word of God in his Proverbs, concerning wisdom. "Get wisdom, get understanding.... Wisdom is the principal thing; therefore, get wisdom: and in all thy getting, get understanding" (Prov. 4:5, 7).

The Hebrew term for wise or wisdom is *chokmaw.* It is used more than three hundred times in the Bible. Therefore, we know that it is very important to God that we get wisdom and employ it in all that we say, and do. Chokmaw has several denotations. It denotes the ability to draw the right conclusion and evaluate a matter correctly. It denotes the kind of decision making which keeps a family, a business, an organization, a nation and it's leadership, on the cutting edge of excellence. The Scriptures tell us in Psalm 33:12 that the nation whose God is the Lord will be a blessed nation. This principle can be applied to any organized body. When God is Lord over a nation, He imparts wisdom to the leaders as they ask for it, and that nation is happy, blessed, and prosperous. Wisdom also exalts a nation. A wise nation is one that is on top. It is ahead of the others. It has a very high rank among the other nations of the world.

Wisdom denotes the ability to perform miraculous signs and wonders such as those performed by Moses before Pharaoh. It denotes the ability to discern the enemy's schemes and plans and locate the weakness in the plan. Through spiritual operations, one has the knowledge and skill to destroy the enemy's plan and confine demonic forces. Wisdom denotes skill and ability in the fine arts, cunning workmanship, and master craftsmanship. It denotes the "wisdom of the ages" transferred from the Ancient of Days into the hearts of men. Wisdom denotes the ability to have and use "common sense."

When God commands us to get wisdom, He is telling us to get the ability to be a righteous judge, learn to evaluate and conclude a matter, get skill and ability in the arts, get the "wisdom of ages," learn to discern who the real enemy is, get some plain, old common sense.[1]

Godly wisdom should be the prerequisite for everything that you set your heart and mind to do. Getting wisdom is the supreme task. It is the first thing that is needed before anything else. If wisdom comes last, expect failure. We do not activate wisdom in our lives often enough. To some, wisdom is a stranger who is entertained a few times out of the year when it is convenient. Still, others make decision after decision, going here and there, doing this and that, and never, for one moment, consider putting wisdom in the forefront of it all. Principal means first, in place, time, order, and rank. It means the beginning, the highest, primary. God is telling us to put wisdom ahead of everything, not just some things that we think, say, and do in life. Our thoughts must be "wisdom thoughts," because what we think, we speak, and what we speak, we will ultimately do. The Bible says, "Through (wise) counsel, make war" (Prov. 20:18). And "In the multitude of (wise) counselors, there is safety" (Prov. 24:6). In other words, get godly wisdom before you undertake any endeavor, great or small.

In Proverbs 3:18, the Bible says wisdom, "Is a tree of life to them that lay hold upon her: and happy is every one that retaineth her." A tree of life is a tree that is planted by a life-giving river of water, not a stream. It brings forth fruit in due season and its leaves do not wither. And whatever this tree does will be very prosperous. This tree described in the first Psalm is the portrait of a wise man, a man who is blessed of God and prosperous. It describes a man who puts wisdom first in his life, making it the principal thing. This man is one who applies understanding and knowledge, because everything that he does prospers. I want to be that man.

STRIFE

Strife is wisdom's mortal enemy. Rather than being filled with the Spirit of God in wisdom, knowledge, and understanding, some individuals are filled with strife, envy, lies, anger, divisions, and malice. Strife comes to oppose wisdom with a vengeance. When God transfers the Spirit of wisdom, strife alerts all of its demonic forces to oppose and hinder the transfer. The Bible says, "The beginning of strife is as when one letteth out water: therefore leave off contention, before it be meddled with. . . . an angry man stirreth up strife, and a furious man aboundeth in transgression" (Prov. 17:14; 29:22), but wisdom works through love.

Strife is one of the most cunning tactics the enemy uses to separate and divide all humanity: mothers and fathers, children and parents, brothers and sisters, employers and employees, leaders and their cabinets, nation against nation, the body of Christ. Strife paralyzes families, corporations, governments, organizations, and the move of God in ministry. Any person who makes strife his or her daily bread is void of understanding.

When strife becomes the principal thing (or principality), in an individual's life, it controls the atmosphere around the person. When this individual is on a team or involved in a group process, for example, the environment is filled with strife. If a member of the team suggests that they should stop their process and begin to seek wisdom regarding the task before them, this suggestion will make absolutely no sense at all to the other team members. In that strife-filled environment, those involved in this group process who are trying to make a good, quality decision will fail. Their decision will cost the company, the family, or the boss an unnecessary loss of money, time, and resources because strife is in control. All efforts to pray and come to a mutual agreement, finalize plans, or conclude the matter will fail.

A minister related the following story. His church was in revival. During the first night of revival, strife had come to oppose the will of God. The minister was not aware of this. He was praying before the revival meeting began. Soon, he asked an intercessor to continue praying, and he also asked another person to continue in prayer after the first intercessor was done. The first intercessor quieted down after a time of prayer. Then, the second one began to pray in the spirit. As she did, the first began to resume prayer, joining the second in what was perceived as harmonious unity prayer. Prayer was flowing smoothly, so he thought. The anointing of God was present to heal the sick. The congregation continued to pray. When prayer ended, the Pastor was introduced and the prayer minister was returning to his seat. To his surprise, and amazement, he was approached in the midst of the worship service by the second intercessor who began to argue and challenge him regarding who he had asked to pray, when, where, and a host of other "wh—" questions regarding pre-service prayer. A spirit of strife entered the service. Miracles did take place that evening by the grace of God. Yet, no one remembered to make an alter call to give ready hearts an opportunity to receive the Savior on this first night of revival.

A few days later, the minister pondered the situation to see how he should handle it. He perceived that the time was not right to approach the person regarding the matter. He began to pray and seek the will of God. He discerned that the devil wanted to create a "big mess." The Lord impressed upon him that he should "forget that mess and get wisdom," because, there is a way, (a thought, an idea, a decision, a plan of action), that "seemeth right unto a man, but the end thereof are the ways of death." But, "When wisdom entereth into thine heart, and knowledge is pleasant unto thy soul; discretion shall preserve thee, understanding shall keep thee: to deliver thee from the way of . . . evil . . . " (Prov. 14:12; 2:10–12, author's paraphrase).

Prayerfully, consider the issues of life and move slowly to resolve them. Do not make haste to speak or to strive. (See Proverbs 25:8; 29:20.) Never rush to judge a person or the offense that he or she has committed.

Not only did the minister "forget the mess," he also "forgave" the person who had trespassed against him for no apparent reason. Notice the wisdom of God, here. God said, forget the mess, not, forgive the transgressor. True forgiveness of a trespass involves forgetting it, first. The proof, or test, of your forgiving a person is found in your forgetting the trespass. You can never really forgive if you do not forget the incident that caused you pain, broke your heart, wounded you, and left you bleeding and dying on the Jericho road, to put it mildly.

Consider this: If you are in Christ, you are a new creation. Therefore you are dead to the former manner in which you conducted your life. (See 1 Corinthians 5:7; 15:31; Galatians 6:15.) And if you are dead, then as a dead man you cannot get upset. Neither can the dead be disturbed, discouraged, intimidated, bothered, irritated, or anything else by life's experiences. The man who is dead to the former pattern of life, serves the Lord and receives a new spiritual life through Jesus Christ" (Rom. 6:11).

Looking back at the story of the prayer minister for a moment, we realize that he suffered embarrassment at the hand of the strife-driven individual. Perhaps you have encountered this kind of personality at a board meeting, committee meeting, the PTA, or the bridge club. The point is this: wisdom kept the minister from "jumping on the strife band wagon" because wisdom will never give strife a position on its team. You should do the same thing. Get wisdom on your team and do not give strife a seat or let it through the door. You can get wisdom, exercise it, and keep it by simply saying, "God, give me wisdom, teach me to use discretion, and help me stay away from strife." Then, God will preserve and protect you from the snare of the enemy. I will discuss strife in more detail later.

---

[1] The definition of wisdom was adopted from the book Hebrew Honey by Al Novac (Houston, TX: J. Coutryman Publishers, 1987, pg. 278).

CHAPTER 3

Here Is Something You Should Know About Wisdom

OD COMMANDS US to get wisdom. (See Proverbs 4:5.) After we are commanded to get wisdom, we are then commanded to get understanding. Understanding is wisdom's seasoning salt. You should not speak bland words of wisdom to resolve issues when you do not know what the issues are, or understand what motivated the major players to do what they did. Without understanding, wisdom is like salt with no flavor. Understanding makes wisdom taste good. No one really likes the taste of food that has no flavor. It is the same way with wisdom. No one really likes or appreciates bland wisdom, but many still partake of it. Understanding sets the tone for an environment in which true wisdom will be received. Whoever partakes of wisdom with understanding will be nourished.

The knowledge of God will guide us into understanding all things, because, "Knowledge of the Holy One is understanding" (Prov. 9:10). It is through faith in God that we understand who He is. As we understand God, we receive the Spirit of God in understanding. Then, when the eyes of our understanding are enlightened by the Spirit of God, we gain not only knowledge of who God is, but insight into the mysteries of God, the kingdom of heaven, and unspeakable joy. Understanding God lays the foundation for understanding all things. It is also the foundation for understanding who we are, why we exist, what our purpose is in life, and how to successfully accomplish our God-ordained destiny.

The Hebrew word for understanding is *biynah*. It means "to separate mentally, to discern, to know." When you get wisdom, and then get understanding, you will be happy and content. Your contentment is based on faith in God.

KNOWLEDGE

Some people have a vast amount of knowledge. They are intellectuals who possess an abundance of information in their field of expertise. However, intellectuals can sometimes be bigheaded, possess little "heart knowledge," or knowledge of the Holy One. Some are always learning, but never really come into the knowledge of the truth. Some have knowledge, but lack wisdom, which is a key ingredient for true success. Without wisdom, a person is unable to transfer knowledge. He is unable to show others that he knows what he knows. He cannot effectively implement a plan to demonstrate what he knows to others. Knowledge was created by God to work in a cooperative relationship with wisdom and understanding. In Proverbs 3:19–20 we read:

> The LORD by wisdom hath founded the earth; by understanding hath He established the heavens. By His knowledge the depths are broken up, and the clouds drop down the dew.

Here we see wisdom, understanding, and knowledge working together cooperatively to establish and complete the work of the Creation. The involvement of all three was necessary to create the heavens and the earth. These three form a triangle, a unified bond. If God found it necessary to employ all three in the great work that brought forth the Creation, how much more should we do the same as we work in the world, in ministry, and in life? Knowledge must be accompanied by wisdom and understanding so that your work and labor of love will produce something that is perfect. A perfect work is a masterpiece. It will bring honor and glory to God.

In our education system we have a wealth of knowledge, but without wisdom and understanding this knowledge is a like bell with no sound. It is like sand, tossed and driven by the wind. The schools of America are full of experts in the field of education. There are educators who have degree after degree in certain areas of expertise. For example, reading specialists graduate from our colleges and universities with masters and doctorate degrees every year. These reading specialists and experts create new and better reading programs. Billions of dollars are spent annually to increase the literacy rate in America. A single school may have several different reading programs, and still, a large number of America's children cannot read or write. The answer to this dilemma is not another degree, not another reading program, not another unnecessary dollar spent on research. The answer is wisdom with knowledge. They will bring understanding into the hearts and minds of our youth. Godly wisdom will speak to the teachers who possess the knowledge, and show them how to get information into the lives of students so that understanding and learning can take place. As we embrace the Son of God through worship, we gain access to the Infinite Source of knowledge, wisdom, and understanding. Faith activates the supernatural database of knowledge.

CHAPTER 4

Carnal Christianity and Wisdom

For they that are after the flesh do mind the things of the flesh; but they that are after the Spirit the things of the Spirit. For to be carnally minded is death; but to be spiritually minded is life and peace. Because the carnal mind is enmity against God: for it is not subject to the law of God, neither indeed can be.

—ROMANS 8:5–7

THE WISDOM THAT God is commanding us to get is from heaven. "But the wisdom that is from above is first pure, then peaceable, gentle, and easy to be intreated, full of mercy and good fruits, without partiality, and without hypocrisy" (James 3:17). Heavenly wisdom is not our own personal brand. It is not based on the principles or doctrine of men. It is God's wisdom—and we need it.

At one time, I was so tired of what I refer to as "CC"s (Carnal Christians) that I did not know what to do. In fact, if a person approached me and identified himself as a believer, mentally I would take my family and distance myself from that person.

In 1 Corinthians 3:1–3, we find a passage in which Paul was speaking to the church about carnality:

And I, brethren, could not speak unto you as unto spiritual, [or as spiritually mature individuals] but as unto carnal, even as unto babes in Christ. I have fed you with milk, and not with meat: for hitherto ye were not able to bear it, neither yet now are ye able. For ye are yet carnal: for whereas there is among you envying, and strife, and divisions, are ye not carnal, and walk as [worldly] men [who are not full of the Spirit of power]?

—1 CORINTHIANS 3:1–3

Paul was much stronger when he wrote to the Romans letting them know that the carnal mind was antagonistic, hateful, and hostile toward God.

I was at a meeting when a discussion came up about a summer missions trip. I had taken some of our youth the previous summer to one of the most beautiful places in the world. I had fond memories of that trip. We had ministered in orphanages, senior citizens complexes, children's emergency hostels, a boy's detention center, a summer school program, and other places. The youth also had an opportunity to spend a week attending a life-changing conference and meet other young people from all over the world.

During the meeting, a "CC" began to talk about the rats in that nation, as she laughed and joked about the missions trip. She showed no compassion for suffering, destitute, less fortunate people, and no concern for the sick that were healed or the souls that were saved. The ambassadorship program she mocked was, first of all, vital to world peace, and, secondly, an encouragement to destitute people around the world. I said in my heart, *Surely Lord, it is alright to rebuke this person, sharply?* I did not wait for God to answer me because I did not really want an answer. I was angry. I rebuked the person and left the meeting. This was a grave mistake on my part. In Proverbs 9:8, the Bible says not to rebuke a mocker. The person will hate you, and gain absolutely nothing from the rebuke. I spoke to the Lord, *It was a test, wasn't it Lord? And I failed it.* This passage of Scripture came to mind:

[Wisdom] is more precious than rubies: and all the things thou canst desire are not to be compared unto her. Length of days is in her right hand; and in her left hand riches and honour.

—PROVERBS 2:15–16

THE WAY OF WISDOM IS PEACE

LENGTH OF DAYS + RICHES + HONOR + PLEASANTNESS + PEACE + MUCH MORE = WISDOM

Once, I was interceding for people to be healed of various sicknesses and diseases (cancer, heart disease, stroke, and arthritis, among others). The anointing of God was once again present to heal. A "CC" walked into the meeting and immediately began to mock and laugh. I continued to pray for God to heal the sick. When prayer was over, I said, *Lord, if I can inflict pain on this "CC" for just a moment, I know that everything will be alright.* My attitude was a mess and, of course, I knew it. I sensed in my spirit the words of Proverbs 24:9, "The thought of foolishness is sin." "You are not wrestling against flesh and blood, but against principalities, powers, ruler of the darkness, wickedness in high places. (See Ephesians 6:12.) These are the demonic powers behind some adversity. I began to realize that wisdom would not fellowship with me because of the kind of attitude I had. The real issue was within me, not the "CC."

I NEED THIS WISDOM

I recently went on a missions trip to the Los Angeles Dream Center. The center had more than 180 outreach ministries at that time, and through hard work they ministered to thousands of needy, less fortunate people each day. We lived on-site at the Dream Center, and although I did not know it at the time of my departure from Michigan, one of my roommates was a "CC." Shortly after we arrived at the Dream Center, her toothpaste was missing and I was accused of stealing it. I ignored the insult openly, but in my heart I said, *Forget the toothpaste! If I am going to steal, it will at least be something of value.* Treasures to be exact—money, precious stones, diamonds, rubies, gold, silver, or expensive artifacts. *Father,* I said, *it is obvious this person thinks her toothpaste qualifies under the category of 'treasure,' but it just does not qualify.* She continued looking for her toothpaste for a couple of days. She never told me if she found it, or realized if she had left it at home. She did not mention her toothpaste again. Well, one day, we went to the grocery store. This same person drove a few of us to the store. She purchased a lot of items, so I decided to help and carry her water to the car. At that point I was accused of attempting to steal her water, even though we were riding back to the Dream Center together, in the same car, and taking the water to the same room at the Dream Center.

I thoroughly enjoyed the time that I spent at the Dream Center, working in evangelism, reaching out to souls in need, and meeting other missionaries from around the world. One of the purposes of wisdom is to confirm who you are in Christ. You may not necessarily know a lot of things, but if you have knowledge of the Holy, and understand who you are and your divine purpose, you have enough knowledge to keep you balanced as you serve the Lord and pursue excellence.

Understanding your purpose and destiny is very important—"CC" or no "CC." There is a cadre of individuals who have put together excellent information on the subject of purpose and destiny that will help you if you have questions regarding who you are, where you fit, and how to use your gifts to glorify God. Your local Christian bookstores, the library, and the Internet should carry some of these materials. When you fulfill your divine destiny as one chosen by God, no "CC" can deter, derail, or overturn the will and power of God. I personally believe that "CC"s come to challenge God's authority that is within you. Wisdom will bring balance as you interact in ministry, in the world, and in life with all kinds of people.

If you are seeking wisdom for the purpose of receiving some new and awesome spiritual revelation, or to elevate yourself to a greater economic and financial status—stop! You and I need wisdom to guide us through life's daily experiences. Appropriately handling the small and simple things in life paves the way to becoming a master over great and unsearchable riches. My encounters with "CC"s encouraged me to revisit wisdom's teachings and look at my own need for a fresh outpouring of wisdom. Wisdom said this,

"He that is slow to anger is better than the mighty; and he that ruleth his [own] spirit than he that taketh a city" (Prov. 16:32). Wisdom wanted me to see and deal with my character, integrity, anger, behavior, and my attitude. I know that I have to consistently work out my own salvation with godly reverence and trembling.

SOME "CC" ENCOUNTERS CANNOT BE UTTERED

As we endeavor to complete our mission in life, we will encounter carnality or immaturity, our own and that of others. Realize that some people want to learn from you, but they do not know how to approach you. I own a plaque that says, "Those who need loving the most, deserve it the least." This is a true saying. Then, there are those who are not for you. They compete when there is no competition in sight. They want to control what you do, based on the standards that they have set for you, and also their perceptions of who you are. Ludicrous—they have no idea who you are. Wisdom will teach you how to be firm and gentle. Balance is the key as we build relationships, and grow in wisdom, knowledge, and understanding.

As I decided to stay balanced in relationships, this scripture came to mind. It was a promise that I was familiar with, one of my favorites:

> For I will take you from among the heathen, and gather you out of all countries, and will bring you into your own land. Then will I sprinkle clean water upon you, and ye shall be clean: from all your filthiness, and from all your idols, will I cleanse you. A new heart also will I give you, and a new spirit will I put within you: and I will take away the stony heart out of your flesh, and I will give you an heart of flesh.
>
> —EZEKIEL 36:24–26

After reading this Scripture, I was more than ready to diligently seek God for wisdom. I was beside myself with excitement. I realized that encounters with "CC"s and other negative experiences in life leave a residue. This is when God reaches down and takes you into His secret chamber and breathes the breath of restoration and resurrection into your life. He encourages you to press on, as He begins to speak His Word. God's Word is like a hammer breaking the residue of negative encounters. (See Jeremiah 23:29.) As He restores the soul with cool, refreshing water, one receives a new heart, a new spirit, and strength for each new day. I am very sure of this one thing—as long as you diligently seek God for wisdom, He will respond in a positive way. He continually gives wisdom. As we draw close to Him, He will continually wash us, heal our wounds, and fill us with a greater depth of wisdom, knowledge, and understanding of the Holy.

CHAPTER 5

Wisdom's True Identity

K NOWLEDGE IS ONE of the greatest assets that we can possess. When we ask God for wisdom, it is important that we know exactly what we are asking God to do for us. What or Who is wisdom? Some equate wisdom with the ability to gain material wealth, fame, and fortune. This connotation of wisdom is based on what we can see and handle though our senses. It is man's doctrine. To take this a step further, some believe that wisdom is synonymous with money and riches gained through either hard work, inheritance, or exploitation. In 1 Kings 3 we find a conversation that takes place between the Lord and Solomon. This conversation reveals the circumstances under which God endued Solomon with wisdom and understanding that would make him the wisest human being ever, past, present, or future. The Lord appeared to Solomon in a dream and asked him what he desired of the Lord. Solomon requested an "understanding heart," not material wealth. He was after something that surpassed the human desire for materialism.

As we pray and ask God to give us wisdom to help our city prosper; wisdom for our president and government; for our children, for our community and schools; for our pastor and those in authority, we must realize that the wisdom of the world will not bring about lasting, positive change. We do not need divine intervention to gain worldly wisdom. However, through the Spirit of God, we will gain wisdom, knowledge, and insight into the things that God gives abundantly and freely. It is not man's wisdom that we are seeking, but it is the wisdom of God that we seek. This wisdom teaches, reveals, and interprets spiritual things to those who live and move by the Spirit of God. God's wisdom will activate positive everlasting change in the world.

I want to make a clear distinction between man's wisdom and the wisdom of God, which is the first item on God's list of true riches. The Scriptures state beyond any doubt who wisdom is. Paul, a New Testament expert on wisdom, declares in his writings to the Corinthians that, "Christ [is] the wisdom of God" (1 Cor. 1:24) and that Christ became wisdom for us (1 Cor. 1:30). Wisdom's true identity is the Christ "in whom are hid all the treasures of wisdom and knowledge" (Col. 2:3). All the treasures of wisdom and knowledge are hidden in Christ, and God is in Christ reconciling us to Himself. So the treasure we seek is Christ, the One who was with the Father from the foundation of the world.

King Solomon received a revelation that wisdom was with the Father from the beginning. Solomon's revelation gives us insight into wisdom's identity. It is found in Proverbs 8:22–31 and is written in the first person:

> The LORD possessed me in the beginning of his way, before his works of old. I was set up from everlasting, from the beginning, or ever the earth was. When there were no depths, I was brought forth; when there were no fountains abounding with water. Before the mountains were settled, before the hills was I brought forth: While as yet he had not made the earth, nor the fields, nor the highest part of the dust of the world. When he prepared the heavens, I was there: when he set a compass upon the face of the depth: When he established the clouds above: when he strengthened the fountains of the deep: When he gave to the sea his decree, that the waters should not pass his commandment: when he appointed the foundations of the earth: Then I was by him, as one brought up with him: and I was

daily his delight, rejoicing always before him; Rejoicing in
the habitable part of his earth; and my delights were with
the sons of men.

Wisdom closes by asking the children of men to pay strict attention to his voice, keep his ways, and apply wisdom on a daily basis.
If they do so, they will be blessed. Finally, wisdom declares that
whoever finds wisdom finds life, and obtains the favor of the Lord.
(See Proverbs 8:32–36.)

John also received a similar revelation of Christ being with the
Father from the beginning, "In the beginning was the Word and
the Word was with God, and the Word was God. . . . All things were
made by him; and without him [wisdom] was not any thing made
that was made. . . . And the Word was made flesh, and dwelt among
us, (and we beheld his glory, the glory as of the only begotten of the
Father,) full of grace and truth" (John 1:1, 3, 14).

When we ask God for wisdom, His desire is to impart within
us the very nature and character of Christ. Even when we do not
ask, God still desires to fill us with wisdom, because Godly wisdom endows a person with the ability to get, enjoy, and maintain
health, success, peace, joy, and love. So, make sure that you understand exactly what you are asking God to do for you. You are asking for an impartation that carries with it a very great and awesome
responsibility. You may think you want wisdom, but can you handle it when you get it? Paul had a "thorn in the flesh" so that men
would not exalt or idealize him because he had an extraordinary
measure of wisdom operating in his life and ministry. He received
an abundance of revelations of God, some of which he could not
speak or utter to another human being. He had the common sense
to give God all of the glory and praise for the wisdom and revelation that he received.

In Paul's epistle to Timothy, he wrote that there is no controversy
over the great mystery of godliness, "God, (Himself) was manifest
in the flesh" (through Christ), and Christ is the wisdom of God.
Amen." (See 1 Timothy 3:16.)

CHRIST, THE WISDOM OF GOD

Whatever Christ did, wherever He went, and whenever He spoke, wisdom, power, and authority were always present with Him. He was, and is, the wisdom of God. All power and authority in heaven and earth have been awarded to Him alone, yet, His words were always presented in simple, commonsense language. He never flaunted His authority. Let's examine the words of Christ when Satan exerted great effort to tempt Him:

1. "It is written, Man shall not live by bread alone, but by every word that proceedeth out of the mouth of God" (Matt. 4:4).

2. "It is written again, Thou shalt not tempt the Lord thy God" (Matt. 4:7).

3. "For it is written, Thou shalt worship the Lord thy God, and him only shalt thou serve" (Matt. 4:10).

Christ sets the greatest example of all, for anyone who desires to operate in the office of wisdom. He gets right to the point, expending minimum time and energy as He speaks to the devil and speaks to us regarding the authority of the Word. It is not so much the words themselves that deliver the message. It is the authority behind them. Through His words, you get a clear picture of the mind of Christ. He understood His destiny and position in life. He knew the exact amount of time He had on earth in order to complete His work and fulfill His mission. Therefore, He did not waste time. If someone was sick, He said, "Be healed." If someone was demon-possessed, He said to the devil, "Come out." If someone was broken-hearted, He had compassion. If someone had lost their way, He said, "Follow me." If someone was dead, He said, "Arise."

Let's examine what the Lord did during these three encounters with Satan:

1. He demonstrated the absolute power and authority of the Word.

2. The Lord spoke the Word boldly to the enemy with absolute power and authority. This was a demonstration of reinforcement of the Word: power of the spoken Word, power of the written Word, and power of the living Word.

3. He did not waver in His approach to defeat the enemy, repeatedly exercising His faith in the Word (three times, to be exact).

When one operates in wisdom authority as Christ does, it is the power and authority that is exerted over the enemy that defeats him. Without wisdom authority, individuals will be put to shame as the enemy exerts power and authority over them.

If you have something to say, and you know what you are talking about, wisdom authority will be released as you speak. Get to the point using language that anyone can understand.

If you are an expert in some area, and you want to share your knowledge with others, do not try to impress anyone with big words. Today, people have a "microwave mentality." If you can take what you have to say and organize it in the same fashion that Jesus did as He spoke to the devil, you will probably have a listening audience. His words are not only simple, powerful, and authoritative, they are the words of His Majesty, the King.

The world is looking for, and needs, someone who can speak and demonstrate the Gospel in beauty and simplicity. There is a hunger and thirst for righteousness no matter what picture the media paints about the state of affairs of this nation or the nations of the world. Darkness covers the earth, and great darkness covers the people, but the grace and love of God are much more abundant than the darkness. People are seeking the Light of the world. They are searching. Some are looking in the right places. What will they hear and see? You hold the key. What will you say and do?

CHAPTER 6

On Sabbatical With God

P AUL WAS ONE of the wisest apostles of the New Testament. One of the great lessons he learned from Wisdom was to be content regardless of his circumstances. He knew how to respond appropriately when he had a lot. He also knew how to survive when he had little. This was a true test of Paul's wisdom. Are you a survivor when your bank account is empty, your stocks are worthless, your home is in foreclosure, and your car has been repossessed? Will you fall apart when you have lost everything, or can you overcome the odds and arise out of difficulty a survivor ready to start life all over again? Wisdom did not pack understanding and knowledge in a suitcase and leave the earth just because you are facing adversity. Wisdom is here. It is alive and well, ministering and working through the Holy Spirit, the Comforter. The earth is full of God's glory. His glory is looking for you.

Paul was a survivor, a man of wisdom, knowledge, and understanding. His contentment and joy were not dependent on material wealth, the accolades of men, his physical surroundings, and most assuredly not on the words and deeds of others who were against him. As a minister of the Gospel, Paul suffered beatings "above measure," (five times he received thirty-nine stripes, and three times he was beaten with rods). He was stoned and involved in three shipwrecks. His life had been in danger many times in the sea. He had been "in perils of water, in perils of robbers, in perils by his own countrymen," and also by the "heathen." He was often in pain, weary, hungry, thirsty, and cold. He was imprisoned more often than his fellow laborers. He was "in deaths," often, yet he survived it all. (See 2 Corinthians 11:24–27.)

He was a brilliant man, writing most of the New Testament. He was a scholar. However, it was the "wisdom connection" that made him great, not his education, nationality, (a citizen of Rome), cultural background, (a Pharisee, the son of a Pharisee), or scholarship. This is the mistake many people make. Believing that the following things make them wise: family or cultural background, education, money, they have become foolish, because things do make some extremely foolish. Everyone should be commended for accomplishments. Things can testify to God's goodness, however these things do not decide or determine whether you are wise or foolish. Sometimes stuff can make a fool of you.

The road to Damascus experience radically changed the way in which Paul viewed life, but his sabbatical connected him to the infinite Source of all wisdom. After receiving his sight, he immediately withdrew himself from other believers and went into Arabia to seek God and get acquainted with Him. He did not confer with any human being regarding the things of God. Paul separated himself from those who had firsthand experience with the Lord. He did not go into Jerusalem to get answers from those who had been apostles before him. He wanted a personal and intimate encounter with the Lord. He did not want another man's opinions of the God who had saved him, healed him, and delivered him from his own destructions. Paul withdrew so that he could behold God's majesty and glory for himself. He wanted God to reveal the mysteries of the kingdom directly to him. He did not settle for an interpreted version of the Christ. For three years he conferred with God and God alone. He was saturated with wisdom and ready to handle the issues he would face from that time forward. It was at the end of his three-year sabbatical that he conferred with his colleagues, going first to see Peter and the other apostles.

Wisdom had fully prepared Paul to handle strife, criticism, jealousy, a broken heart, beatings, betrayal, prison, and his death.

When the voice of wisdom spoke to him during trials and tribulations he recognized it, because for three years he had fasted and prayed, worshiped and adored, communed and fellowshiped with the Lord. During these three years, as Paul got acquainted with God, he gained insight and revelation knowledge into the things of the Spirit. He also understood his call and mission in life. After his conversion, he worked in his calling and gifts, operating in wisdom and the favor of God. Paul understood his life's purpose and divine destiny. Through wisdom, he achieved all he was created to achieve. He carried out his mission with boldness, all the days of his life after his conversion. At the end of his period of being separated unto the Gospel of Jesus Christ, Paul had a good confession and continued to write from prison. He never doubted his mission, no matter how difficult the individual task, or the individuals. He knew that, by the grace of God, Christ would be revealed to the Gentiles through him. During this time, the Lord also revealed to Paul the hardships that he would face and how to handle them. Wisdom taught him how to handle the gainsayers and the game players. Luke 21:15 says, "For I will give you a mouth and wisdom, which all your adversaries shall not be able to gainsay nor resist." At the end of his life, Paul made this statement, "I have fought a good fight, I have finished my course, I have kept the faith" (2 Tim. 4:7).

SPIRITUAL SABBATICALS IN MODERN TIMES

Based on the book *Prayer That Brings Revival*, I concluded that the author is consistently on sabbatical with God and is one of the wisest people in the world today. He is Dr. David Yonggi Cho of Seoul, South Korea. His secret to success is prayer and obedience. He has one of the largest church memberships worldwide with approximately 800,000 members. Dr. Cho spends several hours daily in prayer, fasting, communion, and worship. If his members experience any kind of difficulty, the first thing they do is pray. This is how he and his membership resolve every dilemma they face. Dr. Cho does not necessarily leave his home and go into another city or nation on sabbatical. He nevertheless, withdraws himself as the Apostle Paul did, spending time in fellowship with the Lord. His sabbaticals take place daily. He withdraws, spending the majority of his day in prayerful worship.

I highly recommend the daily sabbatical, spending time in prayer and fasting. You should spend thirty minutes to an hour and more, and begin to pray specifically for an increase in wisdom. You can begin now, praying, "Lord, give me wisdom, because I need it. I want to be saturated with wisdom." If you are disciplined enough to follow simple instructions that may seem out of the ordinary, expect to be enlightened. God's instructions for success may not match your expectations, but if you follow His instructions you can expect to receive an abundance of:

1. Revelation knowledge
2. All of the gifts of the Holy Spirit
3. "God ideas," not just good or great ideas
4. Witty inventions
5. Concepts
6. Insight
7. Power to get wealth
8. Biblical promises fulfilled
9. Honor
10. The favor of God and man

The outcome after conferring with God will surpass your wildest dreams. You can do this! Remember, it must be your desire to obtain wisdom. It will take sacrifice, discipline, and hard work, but it will not be impossible. The wisdom that you need and desire will come through quality time spent in prayer, fasting, worship, word study, and obedience. The benefits will be so extraordinary. Others will stand in awe at what God has done. God will show you the conditions under which you can make such a sacrifice. First, make up your mind. You either want wisdom, knowledge, and understanding, or not. If you do, pray now and ask God to show you His unique plan for your personal wisdom package. Because you are a unique individual, God has an individualized wisdom plan for you with strategies, outcomes, and benefits. I will give you some strategies based on biblical principles that will work every time; but dig deeper, make a diligent search. Elevate yourself to a level of excellence.

MAKE THIS CONFESSION

*The Spirit of excellence is active in my life, right now. I am
full of "God ideas," creative thoughts, insight, and concepts
that I can develop into something that will make the world a
better place. Mankind will benefit from what I do. With men,
things are impossible, but with God, all things are possible.*

Now I want to challenge you to go on a fast, cry out before the
Lord, repent for yourself, your children, your family, and for the
healing of the people of the nations. Ask God to fill you with wisdom. As you pray for yourself and others, I guarantee you that God
will impart wisdom into your heart that will surpass your expectations. Then the Lord will have mercy on you, and your children.
He will forgive you. It does not matter how much money you have,
or what you have accomplished in life, all have sinned, and all need
God's mercy. During this time of fasting, the Lord will do great
things. He will fill you with His Spirit. You will begin to speak and
sing psalms and hymns and spiritual songs, singing and making
music unto the Lord with thanksgiving. It will be a time of praise
and worship, a time of speaking, praying, and singing in the spirit,
a time of rest for the weary soul. "This is the rest wherewith [God]
may cause the weary to rest; and this is the refreshing," (Isa. 28:12),
that will activate wisdom, knowledge, and understanding. (See 1
Corinthians 14:15; Ephesians 5:18–19.)

Once a person has been on sabbatical with God, wisdom, understanding, insight, knowledge, and enlightenment flood the soul.
Does God know you, and do you know Him? This is the position
that Paul was in after basking in the presence of God for three years.
He was known of God, and he knew God. He had spent his time
ministering unto the Lord in the office of a priest. As a matter of
fact, Paul gained so much wisdom and insight, so much knowledge
and understanding—such an "abundance of revelations"—he was
given a messenger of Satan to buffet him. If not, he would have
been exalted above measure because of his wealth of wisdom and
revelation knowledge. God's grace sustained Paul, and in his weakness God's strength was perfected. He was a "chosen vessel unto
(God), to bear His name before the Gentiles, and kings, and the

children of Israel" (Acts 9:15). God does not prefer one person over another. What He did for and through Paul, He will do for you and through you. When wisdom, knowledge, and understanding have become a unified front, and function as a power force in your life, no mess, no test, no strife in life, can stop the Word from exploding within you. Then, you can run through a troop and leap over a wall. (See Psalm 18:29.)

CHAPTER 7

We Need Wisdom, and God Has Given Us Easy Access to It

T HERE IS A very simple formula for acquiring wisdom. In Proverbs 2:6, the Bible says "For the LORD giveth wisdom: out of his mouth cometh knowledge and understanding." He also stores up wisdom for the righteous. This means that God has an exceedingly abundant and unlimited supply of wisdom to give away as gifts to men. Then, He speaks knowledge and understanding to the sharp, focused, and humble listener who has an ear to hear what the Spirit of God is saying. So you must train yourself to become a passionate listener. God is the Giver. You are the one who asks, and you are also the one who receives. All you need to do is tap into the supply of wisdom that has already been made available for the asking. In James 1:5, the Bible tells us that, if any man, woman, or child lacks wisdom, let him ask God for it. And He will give it freely and liberally to them. "For God giveth to a man [what] is good in his sight wisdom, and knowledge, and joy" (Eccles. 2:26). In conclusion, God has already given wisdom, all you need to do is ask for it. As a matter of fact, before you call, He will answer. Wisdom has already been released into the world from the heavenly treasure. You tap into it by asking.

God is eternally looking for someone on whom He can bestow His Spirit in wisdom, knowledge, and understanding. If you love God, that makes you a candidate for wisdom. The desire of God's heart is to fill His people with wisdom, but He has to keep giving it to the children of the world, because they behave themselves wisely. "The children of this world are in their generation wiser than the children of light". (See Luke 16:8.) If any person behaves wisely, God will endow him with even greater wisdom. This is a spiritual principle. It cannot be changed. God is willing to bless His own sons and daughters with an abundance of wisdom. Those who behave wisely will find themselves increasing in wisdom day by day.

God has provided easy access to wisdom because the need for it is so great. There are many reasons why wisdom is not only an asset, but it is a necessity of life. Let's look first at some of the "if clause" wisdom statements found in Proverbs and Psalms that tell why wisdom is an invaluable treasure.

1. Wisdom will preserve you from your enemies, if you
   do not forsake it. In Psalm 121:7–8 we read that, the
   Lord will preserve you from all evil. This means that
   no tragedy, calamity, or plague will come near your
   dwelling. He will preserve you from those who plot
   evil against you. He will preserve you from evil when
   you go out, and when you come in, now, in the future,
   and forever.

WE NEED WISDOM

2. Wisdom will keep you from falling into trouble, if
   you love it. It will keep you in perfect peace of mind.
   In Psalm 121:5, we learn further that the Lord is your
   Keeper who does not sleep or slumber. He is your
   shade on your right. You will not be smitten during
   the day or night.

WE NEED WISDOM

3. Wisdom will bring a promotion if it is exalted. Psalm 75:6 says that promotion comes neither from the east, nor from the west, nor from the south, but God judges and He takes one person down and sets another up in position with new benefits.

FOR A PROMOTION . . . WE NEED WISDOM

4. If it is embraced, wisdom will bring honor. In wisdom's left hand are riches and honor. Riches and honor are with wisdom. (See Proverbs 3:16; 8:18.)

WE NEED WISDOM

5. When you lie down, wisdom will cause you to rest instead of fear. You will not be afraid of sudden fear, and your sleep will be sweet. (See Proverbs 3:24–25.)

DO YOU SEE WHY WE NEED WISDOM?

6. Wisdom will place an ornament of grace on your head. This ornament is God's favor. For it is by grace that we are saved through faith, and it is not of ourselves, but it is God's gift to us. It is His favor. We do not deserve it, but He placed it upon us because He loves us. We are saved by the grace of Wisdom through faith. A wise man obtains God's favor and that favor is seen upon the person's countenance. It looks like a beautiful ornament of gold. Everywhere this wise man goes and whatever he does (according to God's will), God's favor is with him. (See Proverbs 4:9.)

FOR THIS REASON ALONE, WE NEED WISDOM

7. Wisdom will deliver to you a crown of glory. Revelation 2:10 refers to a crown of life that will be given to those who remain faithful through trials and

tribulations, those who overcome the world. A crown of life and glory is the reward for those who are faithful until the end. Wisdom is your assurance that God will find faith when He comes again.

WE NEED WISDOM

8. When a person is open-minded and teachable, he receives the Father's instruction regarding wisdom. The days of his life will be many. The law of wisdom provides, "length of days, and long life, and peace." (Prov. 3:2).

WE NEED IT! DO YOU AGREE?

9. The person who retains wisdom is happy, because wisdom's ways are pleasant. In other words, wisdom never has a bad attitude. And those of understanding always long to be around wisdom. It is like a life-giving tree that nourishes its branches.

SOME MAY NOT AGREE, BUT NEVERTHELESS, WE NEED WISDOM

10. The Bible compares wisdom to honey that is sweet to the taste. When it is found, there shall be a reward and expectation shall not be cut off. The Hebrew term for reward is *achariyth*. It means "future." The word for *expectation* is *tigvah*, and it means "hope," that particular thing for which we long. When we have obtained wisdom, we receive a reward and a sound future. We can anticipate and expect the goodness of God to overshadow us now and in the future. (See Proverbs 24:13–14.)

11. The preceding Scripture also means that our posterity, our future generations, our great, great grandchildren will be wise and will use their inheritance to glorify the Lord. The wisdom seed that we sow in our children and grandchildren will multiply and increase. The

desire to see them become contributors to society and serve the true and living God, instead of squandering their inheritance, will come to pass long after we enter the Father's kingdom.

TODAY, WE NEED WISDOM

12. Wisdom will teach you how to regard, pay attention to, and practice discretion, so that when you speak you will not make a fool of yourself. You will be knowledgeable and the words you speak will be excellent and life producing. When wisdom enters your soul, discretion will preserve you from embarrassment. (See Proverbs 5:2.)

We have all had the experience of standing in a checkout line and hearing the voice of someone telling the family's business. This person wonders why things go wrong, and nothing seems to go right. He or she never recognizes his or her own words as the source of the problem. This person is snared by, and a victim of, his own indiscrete words.

Joseph's positive response to the Virgin Mary had wisdom's signature. When he learned she was pregnant, they were engaged to be married. To suddenly learn that your bride to be is expecting a baby can render you a hard blow, especially if you love her and know that you had nothing to do with her pregnancy. Because the Spirit of God in wisdom was operating in his life, Joseph decided to send Mary away privately and discreetly. He did not embarrass her or her family. Although her miraculous conception of the Lord Jesus Christ had not yet been revealed to him, he still handled his business with discretion. Wisdom had taught him that a man of integrity must handle his business discretely, and not advertise to the whole community that Mary was pregnant before their marriage had been consummated. He kept that business between himself, the Lord, and Mary. What an extraordinary young man.

Today, there is an indiscreet generation who tells stories about their families for financial gain. Children of God do not tell the world your family secrets. People do not want to hear it because they have too many severe, unresolved issues of their own. Go to God in prayer and receive your healing and deliverance. If you find that you need to talk to another human being about your issues, find yourself an excellent Christian counselor. If not, even after the media has paid you for your story, you will have no peace of mind, and more misery and anguish. If someone has committed a crime against you, report it to the proper authorities. If you have a testimony that is going to help someone be transformed into the image of Christ, by all means, tell it.

O, HOW GOD WANTS TO GIVE US WISDOM. AND GUESS WHAT? WE NEED IT, TOO.

13. The Scriptures declare, when wisdom is found, the steps of the righteous will not be hindered. When he runs to take care of God's affairs on earth, he will not stumble, "For a just man falleth seven times, and riseth up again" (Prov. 24:16).

14. "Wisdom is better than weapons of war." (See Ecclesiastes 9:18.) Weapons are necessary because not all men have faith in God's ability to resolve issues, and not all men exercise wisdom. Force will quickly replace wisdom if negotiations fail. Nevertheless, wisdom is superior to weapons of war, and we need it.

Wisdom will teach you how to answer every man, those who love you and those who hate you. Wisdom will show you that for some questions, there are no answers, and for some actions, there are no responses.

"PRECIOUS IN THE SIGHT OF GOD IS THE DEATH OF HIS SAINTS" (PSALM 116:15)

Two men, citizens of the United States, we will call José and Michael, felt compelled to go to a region of the world that had been devastated by tribal war, civil conflict, and was at that time engaged in an all-out war. Both men knew that such a trip was very dangerous. These two men had some things in common. Both had knowledge of the God of Abraham, Isaac, and Jacob. Both loved music. José played the guitar and sang, Michael played violin. Both were brilliant writers. Both were accustomed to taking risks. José was Christian, Michael was Jewish. Both realized the possibility of never seeing their families or friends again. José was told by the UN that he could not travel to this particular part of the world because of the danger. Michael was not restricted because he was a member of the press, and was going on special assignment.

After consideration and planning, each man prepared for his trip. Each left home destined for hostile territory fully focused on his mission. José went to Quetta, Pakistan, and Michael went to Karchi, Pakistan. José was a missionary on official Holy Spirit business. He was an ambassador for Christ. Michael was an award winning journalist.

José was a graduate of Oral Roberts University. He was filled with the Spirit of God in wisdom, knowledge, and understanding. Michael was a graduate of Stanford University, one of the most respected schools in the world. He was an intelligent young man, who was very capable of representing a prominent newspaper.

José's passion to see lost souls saved took him into many nations of the world. Some were open to the Gospel, others were very much "closed" to the Gospel. Michael's passion for reporting news also took him into many nations of the world. I believe that José was moved by the unction of the Holy Spirit, and Michael was moved by a passion to discover a particular truth and complete his research. José was equipped with Bibles, food, and wool blankets to distribute to people in refugee camps. Michael was equipped with journalism gear, perhaps a laptop computer, camcorder, camera, tape recorder, pens, and notepads. José completed his mission in November 2001, delivering food packets, blankets, and Bibles to a refugee camp in Chaman on the border of Pakistan and Afghanistan. Michael was abducted by kidnappers in Karachi, Pakistan, in January 2000. José returned to the U.S. safely after a ten-day trip. He made a second trip to that region delivering winter coats for the children, more food, and more blankets to the people who lived in

Kalli Faizo, a refugee camp in Afghanistan. This man lives in Oklahoma. Michael was the focus of a major search conducted by the FBI and local Pakistani officials. He was martyred.

Both of these brave, courageous men exercised different levels of wisdom, knowledge, and understanding. None of us can determine what a day may bring, but we can live in the spirit daily, asking God to impart His wisdom secrets into our lives. Our enemy is constantly looking for something to steal from someone, someone to kill, and someone's hope to destroy. It does not matter if you are male or female, Jew or Gentile, bond servant or free, young or old, saved or lost.

WISDOM IN RAHAB'S HOUSE

The city of Jericho was closed up and its gates were securely fastened because the Israeli army was prepared for war. It was the seventh day and the seventh time the army of Israel was encompassing the city of Jericho. Seven priests with seven trumpets passed before the Lord. The ark of the covenant, carried also by priests, followed the priests who blew the trumpets. The entire procession was led by the captain of the Lord's host. The captain had revealed himself to Joshua earlier. The people marched behind the ark of God. As they surrounded the city, while the priests blew their trumpets, Joshua commanded the people to shout and they "shouted with a great shout" (Josh. 6:5). As they did, the wall of Jericho fell down. With the wall down, Israel went into Jericho and took the city by force. Joshua was instructed to destroy every living thing in Jericho, both men and women, old and young, as well as the cattle. Something horrible had been going on in "sin city." All were destroyed by the sword. The gold, silver, iron, and brass were taken into the treasury of the house of the Lord. Then, the city was burned.

After the dust settled, the Israelites stood in awe and amazement, for there was one home still standing in the midst of destruction. It did not have a battle scar anywhere. It had not been touched. It was the home with the red thread in the window. The homeowner was Rahab. She had built her home upon the wall. It was not destroyed when the wall fell, or by fire. Neither were the inhabitants of her home destroyed by the sword, or by fire.

Rahab had been called and ordained by God to be a redeemer. Like many of us, she decided to wait until her retirement to answer the call. But time had run out for her. She was about to be destroyed with all of the citizens of Jericho. This life-threatening crisis motivated Rahab to make the right choice. This time, when the call came she answered yes. It was the final call. Her procrastination period had run its course. She made up her mind not to perish with the rest of the inhabitants of Jericho.

She assisted the spies as they gathered information about Jericho. The King of Jericho sent his officers to arrest the spies, but Rahab hid them on her roof and covered them with stalks of flax. I did not think this was a wise thing to do as they could have fallen through the roof or off the roof, but it was indeed a very wise idea. She pretended not to know where the spies were and sent the officers in the opposite direction. She devised a strategic plan of escape for them. First of all, she let them down from the wall through a window of her house. Secondly, she told them to hide in the mountains. Thirdly, she instructed them to remain in hiding for three days. If you can put your wisdom strategy into three easy steps and present it to those who are time-conscious and busy, someone will listen. You can expand it later.

Rahab prophesied to the men about the fall of Jericho, and spoke to them about her plan to save her household, her father and mother, sisters and brothers, and their children from destruction. Rahab was now fulfilling the call of a redeemer, as she discussed the plan to save her family. She entered into an oath of covenant with the spies for her family's salvation, and received a "true token" of their covenant. They gave her a "scarlet thread" to hang in the same window through which they would escape. This thread would identify her home as the only one that would be saved.

Household salvation was only the beginning of Rahab's blessings. God blessed her beyond her imagination. She conceived a son. His name was Boaz. He was born into the royal lineage and house of King David, and therefore Christ. He was the only person in Biblical history who was given the honor of becoming a kinsman-redeemer. As a kinsman-redeemer, he fulfilled the call of God that was upon the life of his mother. This was a very high spiritual office. His father's name was Salmon. "And Salmon begat

Boaz of Rachab; and Boaz begat Obed of Ruth; and Obed begat Jesse; And Jesse begat David the king; and David the king begat Solomon of her that had been the wife of Urias. . . . And Jacob begat Joseph the husband of Mary, of whom was born Jesus, who is called Christ. So all the generations from Abraham to David are fourteen generations; and from David until the carrying away into Babylon are fourteen generations; and from the carrying away into Babylon unto Christ are fourteen generations" (Matt. 1:5–7, 16–17).

If we were to apply today's standards, Rahab and Boaz would have been identified as a dysfunctional family. She was a single parent, but she raised her son in the admonition of the Lord. God delivered them out of dysfunction into royalty. As an adult, Boaz was a wise and prudent man and also very wealthy. He had observed that Ruth, his future wife, had not gone after the young men who worked for him. (Neither had she gone after any man, young or old.) Perhaps, in his youth, Boaz was teased by the other youth in the community about his mother. If so, he would have been sensitive and watchful regarding deviant sexual behavior among his employees. He had not been married before taking Ruth as his wife, and had lived in celibacy in contrast to his mother. Again, I believe that Boaz decided in his youth not to perpetuate his mother's lifestyle.

His handling of the redemption process for Naomi and Ruth astonished all of the witnesses who sat in the gate of the city of Bethlehem. Wisdom had him present his plan in such a way that all of the facts were not disclosed at once. It was a two-part plan, presented in this manner in order to achieve the will of God. Boaz outwitted his enemy. Outwitting the enemy is one denotation of wisdom.

Rahab walked away from the "Jericho wall" lifestyle and the fall of the wall a free woman. The red thread that hung in her window signified the blood of the Passover Lamb, which blotted out the handwriting of her death sentence. She broke the generational curse by the choice she made, and give birth to the generational blessings of the Lord. This blessing states, "The Lord, The Lord God, merciful and gracious, longsuffering, and abundant in goodness and truth, Keeping mercy for thousands, forgiving iniquity and transgression and sin. . . . And shewing mercy unto thousands of them that love me and keep my commandments" (Exod. 34:6–7; Deut. 5:10). Boaz was the fulfillment Rahab's blessing.

Through wisdom, you, too, can walk away from dysfunction into royalty. Obedience is the key. God has a plan that will not only make you functional, but prosper you in everything you do. You must first "get off the wall." Step out of your routine and lifestyle, and step into the Lord's infinitely functional plan with specifications just for you. Here is what you can do to begin: put your ambitions on the back burner. Find someone you can help realize a dream. Then, observe and take notice of your own dreams, moment by moment, season by season, as they become a reality.

CHAPTER 8

OK, I Need It—How Do I Get It?

WHEN YOU ARE born of God, you receive a measure of the Spirit of wisdom, just as Jesus received the anointing of wisdom without measure. (See Isaiah 11:2.) Wisdom comes with the born-again experience. But just as a newborn baby needs care and nurturing, wisdom must be nurtured and nourished by the Word of God in order to grow and mature.

CHILDREN OF THE WORLD

Under certain conditions of grace, God has given the children of this world, (those who are not born of God), wisdom. His purpose is to draw them close to Him so that they may see His glory and realize that true wisdom is a gift from God. However, they do not necessarily use God-given wisdom to bring glory to God. Nevertheless, God chooses the recipients of His grace. He wants everyone to be saved and come into the knowledge of the truth. Therefore, He gives wisdom to the just and the unjust.

PRAYER

A loved one is praying for you to get wisdom. Their prayers are working. I know it, I sense it! Jesus is forever interceding for you.

The Holy Spirit makes intercession for you. Our Father who is in heaven intercedes daily. And our angels stand before God's face on our behalf, awaiting an assignment to minister to those who are called to be heirs of salvation. The power of intercession is working to help you become a very wise and prudent individual.

Paul prayed for the Ephesians to receive spiritual wisdom. He said, "That the God of our Lord Jesus Christ, the Father of glory, may give unto you the spirit of wisdom and revelation in the knowledge of him: the eyes of your understanding being enlightened; that ye may know what is the hope of his calling, and what the riches of the glory of his inheritance in the saints, and what is the exceeding greatness of his power to usward who believe, according to the working of his mighty power, which he wrought in Christ, when he raised him from the dead, and set him at his own right hand in the heavenly places" (Eph. 1:17–20). Prayer is a powerful force. You can overcome anything through prayer.

Paul prayed for the eyes of their understanding to be opened so they would know that God not only had an inheritance of wisdom, knowledge, and understanding for them, but that He had an inheritance in them. We are God's inheritance just as the Ephesians were. We are God's treasure. We can only understand this through the Spirit of wisdom and revelation. Without this revelation, which came through prayer, the Ephesians would not have attained complete fulfillment of their desire to know God. And neither will we.

Prophecy

Paul spoke prophetically regarding his spiritual maturity: "I will come to visions and revelations of the Lord" (2 Cor. 12:1). This is a profound statement that Paul made. He was not bragging, he was stating a fact. Paul was saying that he would gain insight, knowledge, and understanding into the things of the Spirit of God. He was able to say this without reservation or boasting because he had spent time in God's presence. You must declare the same things. Say it with power and authority in your voice, "I will come to visions and revelations of God."

Desire

If your heart's desire is to be wise and prudent, overflowing in knowledge and understanding, then you should carefully consider doing the following:

1. Cease from your own wisdom. (See Proverbs 23:4.) A person who is caught up in his own wisdom knows everything. You cannot tell him anything. He knows it all. The pride in his heart is so thick, there is no room for God's wisdom. The kingdoms of his heart are full of himself. Do not bother telling this person anything. He will not receive from God and neither will he receive from you. If you are this kind of person, repent, and cease from your own wisdom.

2. "Trust in the LORD with all thine heart; and lean not unto thine own understanding. In all thy ways acknowledge him, and he shall direct thy paths" (Prov. 3:5–6). God will instruct you and teach you in the way that you should go. He will guide you and monitor your progress.

3. "Be not wise in thine own eyes: fear the LORD, and depart from evil" (Prov. 3:7).

4. Do not reject or look down on wisdom. Do not reject good advice.

5. Do not forsake or get away from wisdom. Stick with wisdom. Keep searching for it and seeking it.

6. Love wisdom above all things.

7. Highly esteem and exalt wisdom.

8. Embrace wisdom.

9. Love and enjoy instruction. Always remain teachable. Be a learner.

10. Worship. Do not complain, find fault, or murmur.

11. Commune and fellowship with the Lord daily in prayer. Fast regularly.

12. Let others commend and praise you, never praise yourself.

13. Read Proverbs daily and follow the instructions you read.

THE WISDOM TRANSFER

Wisdom like faith is composed of spiritual substance. When God fills a person with the Spirit of God in wisdom, knowledge, and understanding, a divine revelation of God from God is transferred into a person's life. During this transference of power, wisdom moves from its supernatural existence in Christ into a human spirit, which is born of God. As I mentioned earlier, under certain conditions of grace, the children of this world also receive a certain measure of God's wisdom. (See Luke 16:8.)

When wisdom moves from its heavenly existence into the earth, it must be received by the spirit of man because the natural man cannot and does not receive the things of the Spirit of God. The things of God are foolishness to the natural man. The natural man cannot know and understand the things of God because they are spiritually discerned. With the transference of wisdom also comes revelation knowledge of the Holy One. A person is then able to really know and experience the love of Christ. This love fills us with the fullness of God in many ways, which include, but are not limited to, power, virtue, insight, character, joy, love, hope, faith, and peace. (See 1 Corinthians 2:14; Ephesians 2:14.) Will you feel something happen to you when wisdom is transferred into your spirit? You may or you may not, but you will certainly think, speak, and act differently.

YOU MUST BE QUALIFIED FOR THE TRANSFER

First of all, a fool will not receive wisdom. The Bible says, "The fool has said in his heart there is no God" (Ps. 14:1). "Fools [also] hate knowledge" (Prov. 1:22). Therefore, the fool will not receive something from Someone Who in his mind does not exist. When the fool hears the Gospel preached, he says to himself, "What God? There is no God." His heart is stony. Now, you cannot be a fool and expect to receive the Spirit of wisdom and revelation in the knowledge of God. If you are a fool, you should not expect to receive anything from God's treasury. Because a fool hates knowledge, he will not receive wisdom or understanding. However, a person of understanding already has wisdom.

Secondly, fear of the Lord is the beginning of wisdom. (See Proverbs 1:7.) Without fear of the Lord, the door to wisdom is locked. When a person acknowledges that God alone is the infinite Creator, recognizes that He is the Omniscient, Omnipotent, and Omnipresent One, when he honors, respects, reveres, and loves God, the Lord will bring that person into the beginning stages of wisdom development. It is obvious to me that the children of the world have tapped into this principle. They may not shout about their godly reverence to the world, but in their secret place, they reverently fear the Lord. Wise worldly individuals do experience certain levels of wisdom. Remember, however, that wisdom is spiritual treasure. It cannot be transformed, translated, or condensed into man's doctrine, but when God is exalted, highly esteemed, and adored, wisdom is in full operation.

Wisdom is initiated in a person's heart only when God is revered. The fear of the Lord is treasure to the wise, it is clean, enduring forever. (See Isaiah 33:6; Psalm 19:9.) Godly reverence is the key that unlocks the door to the Spirit of God in wisdom. Then, revelation knowledge and understanding can enter because the door is open. The fear of the Lord is pure and holy. It purifies and cleanses the soul and fulfills the desire to live a clean, holy, and righteous life. In an environment of righteousness wisdom flows freely.

Thirdly, you must understand that God just simply gives the gift of wisdom. (See James 1:5; Proverbs 2:6.) He will not give you a counterfeit. If you ask Him for wisdom, He will not give you confusion. The Bible says, if you know how to give good gifts to your children, how much more will God give the Spirit of God in wisdom to those who ask? Gifts are given because of love. You do not earn gifts. The giver wants to express love and appreciation to the receiver through the gift.

Fourthly, the Bible says if anyone lacks wisdom, he should ask God for it. (See James 1:5.) Some people prefer to ask astrologers, stargazers, and prognosticators, but I prefer to ask God. Some are too proud to ask. And others do not know how to come to God with an attitude of humility. When you humbly ask for wisdom, God will fulfill your request. Asking indicates a receptive heart and mind:

> Ask, and it shall be given you; seek, and ye shall find; knock, and it shall be opened unto you: For every one that asketh receiveth; and he that seeketh findeth; and to him that knocketh it shall be opened.
>
> —MATTHEW 7:7–8

Finally, the giver of the gift must have a wiling receiver. If you say with your mouth that you want wisdom, but you do not believe you will receive it, then you will not. But if you believe that you will receive wisdom when you ask God for it, then you will receive it. The receiver must believe that God rewards those who wholeheartedly ask, and seek Him through faith.

YOU MAY BE A VESSEL THROUGH WHOM GOD TRANSFERS WISDOM TO OTHERS

Once you have received wisdom, you can transfer wisdom to others. Let me explain by an example. Our congregation believed that fellowship with other ministries edified the body of Christ. We would go regularly to visit other churches. Our entire congregation is involved in outreach, as we went to bless another church with praise and worship, prayer, preaching the word, and other ministry gifts.

This particular outreach took place on a beautiful fall Sunday morning. The leaves on the trees were bright red, orange, yellow, and brown. The birds were still singing, but I knew they were preparing to fly south very soon. The city streets were quiet, not a lot of traffic as we drove to the church. This Sunday, I was a few minutes late getting to the service. When I arrived, before I could take my coat off, someone in authority asked me to lay hands on the keyboard. I could sense that this person was troubled because praise and worship had not begun.

I did not say a word as I proceeded to the keyboard. The worship leader was an accomplished musician and worshiper who understood the complicated mechanism of a sound system. She was sitting at the keyboard perplexed, pressing this button, that button, but there was no sound. The soundman was checking wires and connections, going from the keyboard back to the sound system, checking more wires and adapters. He had made a thorough check. Still, there was no sound. I assumed this had been going on for about ten minutes. The two congregations were waiting, some members impatiently, for praise and worship to begin. With these two congregations as witnesses, a senior leader wanted me to lay hands on a keyboard that would not make a sound.

Well, I walked up there as though I laid my hands on keyboards everyday. I did not look at the congregation, the worship leader, or the soundman. I laid my hands on the keyboard, and said, "Father, give the worship leader and the soundman wisdom in the name of Jesus." I bound the devil, and loosed the will of God. I prayed in the Spirit for a few minutes. In three or four minutes, the most beautiful music began to fill the sanctuary. It was a familiar sound. The congregation was being led into praise and worship. Very soon, everyone's attention was focused on the Lord. Was wisdom released as I laid hands on the keyboard into the keyboard? No—objects do not need wisdom, people do. Wisdom was released into the heart of the worship leader and the soundman. Whoever needed it, as I spoke to God on their behalf, received it.

What did I learn from Wisdom and about wisdom that day? First of all, God will make an unusual request when you least expect it. You really may not know what to do. You may think that you look ridiculous doing what has been requested, and as you consider it, it is ridiculous. But obedience is key. I did what I was instructed to do. I was shocked when I heard music flowing from the keyboard so quickly. I knew that I was not responsible for what had happened. To this day, I do not know what happened. I did not ask anyone anything. Was it a miracle? Yes, it was. Did God transfer wisdom to either the soundman, the worship leader, or both, so that the right adjustment could be made to the sound system? Yes, God transferred wisdom, because that was the request He put in my heart. That day, God wanted to transfer wisdom and He did. I was a key player in the transfer. I do not know why! God could have transferred wisdom directly to whom ever He wanted, but He did not.

Also, when a person is an expert in an area, he or she will tend to lean to their own understanding, when God wants their dependence on Him. There may have been a technical problem with the equipment, but with God the issue was wisdom. When I responded positively to the request, I had no idea what I would ask God to do. The wisdom that the receiver got that day was not for that time only. It will last through out eternity. They can tap into it at any time.

CHAPTER 9

Stay Free

The servant of the Lord must not strive.

—2 TIMOTHY 2:24

ONE DAY, I was relaxing, studying, and minding my own business, when Wisdom began to speak to me, *Strife is the enemy of God, of wisdom, and of freedom.* "Stand fast therefore in the liberty wherewith Christ hath made us free, and be not entangled again with the yoke of bondage" (Gal. 5:1). Wisdom continued to speak, *Your freedom was not bought without a price. It was not cheap. It cost the Father the life of His one and only Son. God purchased your freedom, and the payment was the blood of Jesus Christ. People will not necessarily encourage or celebrate you. The truth is, they will hate you because of the Gospel and because of Christ. If they hated Me, then, they will also hate you. Learn to encourage yourself in the Lord at all times. You must remain strong in the Lord and in the power of His might. Always let My joy be your strength.*

DON'T GET CANCER!

Wisdom continued, *Do not allow strife, a cancer-causing agent, to bring you to an early grave. Most people believe cancer is a physically debilitating disease. This is true, but it begins in the emotions and finishes in the physical body, working to destroy human life.*

As I was meditating on Wisdom's words, "Don't get cancer," I began to think about one of my visits to the doctor. I needed a physical examination and I wanted an alternative medical examination. I decided to go to the world-renowned Oasis of Hope Hospital in beautiful Tijuana, Mexico. During my medical treatment, I had an excellent medical team caring for me. I also met wonderful people from all over the world who had come for treatment. Most of them were critically ill. They had come to Oasis of Hope after all hope was gone. Before coming to Oasis, many of the patients had had repeated surgeries and chemotherapy and still the cancer had come back to haunt them, attacking other parts of their bodies (liver, lungs, brain, neck, spine) which were not the original site of the cancer.

I questioned the Lord regarding these patients. Why had they waited until the final stages of the disease to seek alternative treatment? Why didn't they come at the onset of the disease, or when they first learned of their condition?

You can seek wisdom now, or you can seek it after disaster. But if you get it first, and put it first, you can avoid disaster.

STRIFE IS LIKE CANCER, IT HAS A HIDDEN AGENDA

> For where envying and strife is, there is confusion, and every evil work.
>
> —JAMES 3:16

Evil work is a demonic power, and the love (and control) of money (any and everybody's) is the root of evil work. (See 1 Timothy 6:10.) It functions like a corporation, and evil work is the CEO. Confusion, envy, and strife are board members. Envy and strife are two separate demonic forces, but they are in partnership working very closely together. They are the doorkeepers for the major corporation of demonic powers known as evil work. They are not a major force in the network. They open the door for evil work. When they have control of a person, they call stronger forces to back them up. I will list some of these evil works for whom envy and strife open the door. (See Romans 1–3.)

Envy and strife open the door for hatred of truth. It causes individuals to rebel against the truth, hinder it, interfere with it, and suppress it. Even though God has revealed Himself through the Creation, He is not glorified, given thanks, honored, or revered as God. He is hated. Hatred of the truth makes the truth of God appear as a lie, and calls a lie the truth.

Envy and strife invite vain imaginations in until the heart of the captive is full of darkness. They make a person believe and confess that he or she is wise, when in reality that person has become a fool. The person gets carried away with his imagination. This individual, for example, will worship idols rather than worship God, the Creator.

Evil work's co-workers cause men and women to engage in all forms of ungodliness and uncleanness through lust, to dishonor their bodies having vile and unnatural affections, and to become reprobate in their thinking. Here is a list of some of evil works other co-workers:

- wrath
- debate
- fornication
- sickness
- backbiting
- disease
- whispering
- depression
- mental illness
- insanity
- adultery
- unrighteousness
- maliciousness
- murder
- divisions
- inventors of evil things
- spiteful
- out of control
- "full of the devil"
- malignity

The goal of strife is to open the door to the final and progressive stages of evil work, which is destruction through malignity. Evil work destroys a person emotionally, psychologically, and physically, and can cause physical and spiritual death. If strife is allowed to take control of one's thinking and actions, a decision has been made to open the door to the progressive and final stages of strife. Please realize that strife does not work alone. Its partner is envy. Envy holds the door open for many of its friends and co-laborers. This is dangerous.

Evil work does not work alone. Confusion is chairman of the evil work board. In the midst of the evil work there is a spirit of confusion. Another danger is that evil workers deceive one another, but they themselves are also being deceived by the master of deception. Before they know it, they have been taken captive to a place they never intended to go. They never find a way of escape, or ever take hold of the path of life again. Once, I was on my way to that place of "no return," when suddenly, wisdom instructed me to *Stop!*

To the natural mind, it does not seem possible that strife can lead a person into so much evil work. Every person who is under the influence of the spirit of strife may not be involved in all of the works of evil, but they will be involved in some of the works of evil. The enemy knows the destruction God has delivered a person from, because the enemy is the destroyer. Satan will plot to give evil work access into your life through strife.

Some day, however, when the workers of iniquity least expect it, every evil work will be judged and sentenced. Because the sentence against evil work is not executed quickly, the hearts of many people are fully set on doing evil. The days of the sinner may be prolonged, but the day of judgment for evil work will come. In the time of judgment, all will be well with those who fear the Lord, "But it shall not be well with the wicked . . . because he feareth not before God" (Eccles. 8:13).

It is important that you stay free of strife so that the wells of wisdom can flow continually. Strife will abruptly stop the wisdom flow. Make up your mind, make a positive decision, that you will stay free of every evil work and the workers of iniquity. Do not be a partaker in another man's sin. Get some new associates and do not be quick to call just anyone your friend. Choose your friends carefully and stand strong and firm, immovable in the liberty wherewith Christ has set you free:

> When offense comes,
> "STAY FREE!"

> When others talk about you behind your back,
> "STAY FREE!"

> When people say all manner of evil against you,
> "STAY FREE!"

> When the thief steals from you,
> "STAY FREE!"

> When all hell breaks loose,
> "STAY FREE!"

> When criticism comes against all you do,
> "STAY FREE!"

> When you are judged unfairly,
> "STAY FREE!"

> When that fault-finding spirit rises up,
> Encourage yourself in the Lord, and
> "STAY FREE!"

> When you are misunderstood,
> "STAY FREE!"

> When others mock the Spirit of God,
> "STAY FREE!"

> When all hope is gone,
> "STAY FREE!"

> When test, trials, and tribulations come,
> "STAY FREE!"

When the enemy comes to steal, kill, and destroy,
"STAY FREE!"

Blessed are ye, when men shall revile you, and persecute
you, and shall say all manner of evil against you falsely,
for my sake. Rejoice, and be exceeding glad: for great is
your reward in heaven: for so persecuted they the prophets
which were before you.

—MATTHEW 5:11–12

UNDER THESE CONDITIONS YOU CAN "STAY FREE"

I cannot stress enough the importance of your freedom. You cannot
hear the voice of Wisdom speak words of life and power when you
are in bondage. God wants to translate you by His Spirit to a place
where others will not go to preach the Gospel, and set the captives
free. For this special trip you will not need jet service. You will take
flight with the Holy Spirit if you will stay free. However, if you are
in bondage, you are the captive, the one who needs to be set free.

Wisdom is one of the Father's free agents, who was established
before the foundation of the world. Wisdom will not move into a
life that is in any kind of bondage. However, when the Son of God
sets you free...

YOU ARE ETERNALLY FREE

After Christ has liberated you, you should never allow the love of
God to grow cold because of the issues of life. God's love will give
you peace of mind regardless of your circumstances. This is how the
Scriptures describe God's love: God's agape love suffers long and is
kind. It is not envious. It is not selfish, does not act up, does not
provoke or think evil, is glad when truth prevails, and it bears all
things and keeps hoping in all situations. Love endures everything
that happens, and it never, ever fails. (See 1 Corinthians 13.)

CHAPTER 10

Even When You Are in a Rut, Wisdom Will Rescue You

MERCY EXISTS WITH wisdom. Sometimes, because of hardship, extreme misfortune, and destitution, an individual cannot receive the wisdom that God is transferring to them. Nevertheless, God has a wisdom strategy that will deliver any person out of the most severe circumstances. Because of the extreme nature of an individual's present circumstances and physical surroundings, their primary focus is simply day-to-day survival. They cannot even see the light of day, and they certainly are not in the frame of mind to receive enlightenment from the voice of wisdom.

Such was the case with the Israelites 1,491 years before the birth of Christ. The people of Israel had been in Egyptian bondage and slavery for 430 years. It was a perpetual family curse that had continued, generation after generation. This curse of slavery was passed on, and thus was inherited by each succeeding generation. The people just did not know what to do. They had lost all hope of ever being free. Slavery had captivated their minds and emotions, as well as every aspect of their being. They did not even think clearly or rationally like free men. Being under a cruel and evil taskmaster like the Pharaoh could literally drive a person insane.

Slavery had almost destroyed their, hope, their vision, and even their faith. Therefore, God had to reach outside of their familiar surroundings and find a person through whom He could transfer wisdom to His people.

God had enlightened Moses and prepared him for the rescue. He was the wisdom of God moving and ministering among a people who believed their posterity began and ended in slavery. Moses had his hands full. The people had not had a deliverer in 430 years, and they did not really want one. Sure, they had dreamt of their freedom, but they believed that such an escape from slavery into freedom was just an impossible dream. When you are void of wisdom and understanding, you think that the mess you are in is pretty good, because this is all you know. Fortunately for the Israelites of the Old Covenant and for us today, who are living under a new and better covenant, the wisdom plan of God has never involved slavery. As a matter of fact, God hates slavery—physical slavery and slavery to sin.

The Bible says that the children of Israel had taken a journey into Egypt to escape the famine in their homeland. Before going into Egypt, they were a free people and had moved to the land of Goshen temporarily. They were a small nation, Jacob and his twelve sons and their families. They had no intention of staying in Egypt permanently, and they certainly had not anticipated becoming slaves.

The Israelites were very successful and prosperous. They had multiplied and became very great in number while in Egypt. Then, a new Pharaoh who did not know Joseph came into power. The Egyptian ruler and his government envied Israel when they saw how wonderfully God had blessed them. However, during that 430 years of captivity, something extraordinary happened. The few of them who took the journey into Egypt became a great multitude of people. God increased them in strength and fortitude. They were diligent, hardworking people, working fifteen to twenty hours a day without clean water to drink. Still, they increased and multiplied. Did they realize that their survival was a miraculous work of God?

The Israelites did not believe that they had the wisdom, power, or knowledge to bring themselves out of slavery. Wisdom had to make a way for them working outside the camp on their behalf.

Wisdom had planned their rescue and escape from slavery before the foundation of the world. A wisdom strategy had already been created just for them. It is called the Passover. God has a wisdom strategy to bring you out of the dire state of affairs that have overshadowed the will of God for you. Not only that, God has a wisdom strategy to save those who have been involved in the plan of destruction for your life. It is a seven-step wisdom strategy to save them—if they will hear and obey the voice of wisdom.

On the eve of the Passover the wisdom of God was beginning to speak and move, positioning the Israelites for the great escape. Shortly before midnight, Pharaoh woke up and he saw what had happened. The Spirit of the Lord, who is rich in wisdom, knowledge, and understanding caused Pharaoh to call for Moses and Aaron. It was by God's commandment, not of his own volition, that Pharaoh told the Jewish people they could go and serve their God. Pharaoh, his servants, and all the Egyptian people woke up during the night. Every Egyptian household had at least one person who had died as a result of the plague. There was much crying in Egypt that night. Here we see mercy operating with wisdom. All the members of the household of each Egyptian family could have been destroyed, but they were not.

"And (Pharaoh) called for Moses and Aaron by night, and said, rise up and get you forth from among my people, both ye and the children of Israel; and go serve the Lord as ye have said. Also take your flocks and your herds, as ye have said and be gone; and bless me also" (Exod. 12:31–32). God's enemy always wants the blessings of God, but not God's wisdom. In essence, the enemy wants the blessing, but not the God of the blessing. Pharaoh had entertained the wisdom and blessing of God on at least seven different occasions in the face of the man Moses before the Passover. He had ample opportunity to gain wisdom, knowledge, and understanding, as well as receive seven blessings from God, rather than positioning himself for seven plagues. He could have saved himself and his people from destruction. Each time God sent His humble servant Moses to Pharaoh, Moses presented him the plan of salvation. Seven times, Pharaoh refused salvation and rejected wisdom. He gave his permission instead for a plague to destroy his people and the land. His pride, arrogance, witchcraft, and his desire to control another person's life paved the way to his own destruction.

Sometimes, when gifts and blessings are presented to a person, he or she quickly moves to judge the manner in which the gift is wrapped, rather than opening the gift and examining the contents. This is what Pharaoh did. Seven times he judged the blessings of God as unworthy of his acceptance because Moses was not dressed in royal attire. Moses just did not look like someone who could be a blessing, or present a blessing to anyone. Pharaoh was still asking for the blessing that God had already sent to him seven times. He wanted the blessing and the one presenting it to fit his great expectation.

The Egyptians were very anxious for the Israelites to leave their country, after the death of all their firstborn. They prepared to send them away in a hurry because they thought they were all going to die. The Israelites took their unleavened bread and kneading troughs and rolled them up in their clothes. Placing their goods on their shoulders, they began the exodus out of slavery.

Suddenly, as they were leaving, miraculous power began to move in their midst. Notice what happened: God put it into their hearts to ask the Egyptians for their possessions. Because their slavery had been reversed, Israel was now in a position of authority. It did not take them long to command the Egyptians to give them gold and silver and fine clothing. So, when they left Egypt, they did not just go away, they went out with their multitude of flocks and herds, jewels of gold and silver, and fine new clothes. All of this took place within the same day. The Israelites went from bondage into abundant living. They stepped out of slavery, out of emotional, psychological, and physical bondage into a new life within twenty-four hours. Unable to help themselves, and void of a wisdom strategy of their own, the Israelites managed to go "from rags to riches" all within the same day. Did they ask God to make them wealthy as they left Egypt? No. Their main concern was the Exodus—safely escaping out of the hands of the Pharaoh:

> Now the sojourning of the children of Israel, who dwelt in Egypt, was four hundred and thirty years. And it came to pass at the end of the four hundred and thirty years, even the selfsame day it came to pass, that all the hosts of the LORD went out from the land of Egypt. It is a night to

be much observed unto the LORD for bringing them out from the land of Egypt: this is that night of the LORD to be observed of all the children of Israel in their generations.

—EXODUS 12:40–42

I believe this story was recorded to encourage someone. Can you get a vision of God working with one of His special wisdom agents to be instrumental in your deliverance? The story of the Exodus is not a fairy tale, but a true event in history. God brought Israel out of bondage and changed their lives forever. Someone is about to step out of bondage into a brand new lifestyle within the same day. The only thing you need is desire. You do not even need wisdom. God is working His wisdom outside of you, for you. The windows of heaven are opening up for you because God can trust you to fulfill the work of the kingdom of God. You are thinking, how can this be? You must understand that spiritual things are spiritually discerned. It is time to wake up; shake yourself and expect the unexpected, expect the supernatural—expect a miracle.

THE ART OF INTERCESSION

Now, let's see specifically what the children of Israel did to move God with compassion and cause Him to send Moses, a man of wisdom and power, to deliver them out of the hand of their enemy. We know that as slaves, the Israelites did not believe they had the wisdom, knowledge, or power to strategize their escape. They did have intercessors in the camp, who understood the power of prayer. If you do not have the wisdom and power that you need for your own deliverance, intercession will work. As a matter of fact, the art of intercession is one of the most powerful wisdom strategies God ever created. Jesus is ever interceding for you and me. Once intercession is activated it will result in dramatic change, as seen in the story of the Exodus.

Sometime during the final years of their 430 years of captivity, the intercessors realized that if they did not pray fervently, they would be Pharaoh's slaves forever. The Bible says in Exodus 2:23–25, "the children of Israel sighed by reason of the bondage, and they cried, and their cry came up unto God by reason of the bondage. And God heard their groaning, and remembered his covenant with Abraham, with Isaac, and with Jacob. And God looked upon the children of Israel, and respected them," and He delivered them.

There were the three components of Israel's intercession. They 1.) sighed, 2.) cried, and 3.) groaned. The Israelite's sighing, crying, and groaning may not appear to be the sound of wisdom, knowledge, and understanding because we associate wisdom with eloquent words, and excellence in speech and linguistic ability. However, wisdom is the supernatural ability in the spirit of a man to solve problems, resolve conflict, and establish stability and harmony in a righteous, godly manner. The noise Israel made to God was music to His ear. It was the song of wisdom, and deliverance, and sincere longing to be free. It was this wisdom that initiated the Passover and the Exodus, and coming out with a thousand times more soul prosperity, spiritual prosperity, and economic prosperity than they had ever possessed. As they groaned, the Spirit of God began to help them pray, with groaning that could not be understood. The Bible says the Holy Spirit will assist us in our prayers and this is what happened to them. (See Romans 8:26–27.) Once the Holy Spirit began to help the intercessors pray according to the will of God, God knew that their hearts were pure. They did not know how to pray specifically for their deliverance, so the Spirit of God helped them pray for the deliverance of the entire congregation.

The Hebrew term for intercession is *paga*, and it means "one who falls on his face before God, meeting together with God, entreating God, while also coming against the powers of darkness." It also means running to God on behalf of the lost, the hurting, the offended, and the dying until God hears and answers prayers of desperation and sincerity, and blesses the people. In Psalm 102:17, the Bible says that the Lord, "will regard the prayer of the destitute, and not despise their prayer." These people were certainly in a state of destitution when the intercessors made their appeal to the Lord. If you are impoverished, less fortunate, or destitute, you are in the right position for God to give you a same day, rags to riches miracle. Do not stop praying and interceding. When you think you have no wisdom, knowledge, or understanding to help yourself get out of a rut, if you can just intercede you are on your way to recovery. It was not just idle sighing, crying, and groaning that was offered to the Lord, because you can shout, holler, scream, cry, beg, and have a temper tantrum and still not move God with compassion. Their sound was directed to and focused on God. It was sincere and heartfelt. It was the sound of true intercession. Intercession was their wisdom strategy and it can also be yours. This strategy caused God to send Moses, the deliverer, institute the Passover, and initiate the Exodus. Intercession is one of the most powerful forces in the universe. And it will bring unprecedented change into existence.

The wisdom strategy of intercession initiated twelve miraculous events that brought fulfillment of the Passover and Exodus for the children of Israel, as they obeyed the commandments of God through Moses:

1. God performed great signs and wonders in the presence of the enemies (Ps. 105:28–36).

2. The Passover saved the Jews from destruction (Exod. 12:13, 23, 27).

3. There was freedom and liberation from slavery. The Bible says if you serve sin you are a slave to sin. The Jewish nation was in physical slavery, but we can also be enslaved by sin. The sinner is held captive by the invisible slave-owner. But when God says, "Satan, let my people go," sin has to release the captive just as Pharaoh had to release the children of Israel and let them go free (Exod. 12:28, 31, 33).

4. There was divine health among the people. The Bible states that there was no sick, feeble, or depressed person among the Jews when they came out of Egypt. If you work for a taskmaster who is repeatedly beating you, not allowing you to take a break and get water, who forces you to work fifteen to twenty hours a day under unsanitary conditions, you should be feeble, sick, depressed, and insane. They were not depressed,

they were not feeble, they were not sick, and they were not insane (Ps. 105:37).

5. Their personal needs were met when they were out in the wilderness. God provided manna for food and He provided water. He also provided quail. This was all done by supernatural provision (Exod. 12:36; 15:25; Ps. 105:40–42).

6. Prosperity and wealth came into their hands. They received a great spoil. Their own flocks and herds had multiplied, they had food, clothing, and beautiful raiment. They received silver and gold in abundance (Exod. 12:32, 34–36).

7. They had divine protection during the Exodus. There was a cloud by day to protect them from the heat of the sun and other dangers. This cloud at one time was a wall of separation between the Egyptians and the Israelites allowing time to escape Pharaoh's destructive intentions. When the cloud appeared, it was dark on the Egyptians side, but there was light on Israel's side (Ps. 105:39).

8. God increased the numbers of His people making them greater than their enemies. A few went to Egypt, but approximately three million souls came out—men, women, children, and a mixed multitude (Ps. 105:24).

9. Revival broke out and God brought them forth with joy and gladness (Ps. 105:43).

10. Restoration. Not only did they get to keep their own possessions, God gave them the land of the heathen and they inherited things that the heathen had labored for and gathered (Ps. 105:44).

11. The miracle of the dry land. God performed an awesome miracle: when Israel crossed the Red Sea.

The water stood up on both sides of the sea and they walked in the midst of the sea on dry dusty land. The bottom of the sea was not even muddy (Exod. 14:21–22).

12. Total destruction came upon their enemies who were drowned in the sea while pursing them (Exod. 14:28).

Part II:
Worship

CHAPTER 11

The Divine Connection: If You Want to Be Saturated With Wisdom, Worship God

THERE IS A divine connection between wisdom and worship. Wisdom will lead you into godly worship. However, worship will cause you to increase in wisdom more and more. More worship, more wisdom—more wisdom, more worship. The more you worship God, the more you will be filled with wisdom and revelation knowledge of God. If you are wise, you will worship God. A true worshiper will increase in worship and in wisdom. Right now, in this very hour, the Father is looking for true worshipers, those who will worship Him in spirit and in truth. God is Spirit and those who worship Him must worship Him in spirit and in truth. (See John 4:23.) When the true worshiper worships the Father in truth there is nothing that the worshiper tries to hide from God about himself. God knows all things. Yet, He expects the one who seeks Him to confess his or her faults and sins openly and honestly so that He can cleanse them from all unrighteousness. To worship God in the spirit means "to commune and fellowship with Him through the human spirit." It is not through ability, senses, the mind, or our emotions that we worship God. Studying and meditating in the

Scriptures prepares the way for communicating with God through the spirit. God has prepared marvelous and unsearchable things for those who love Him. He only reveals these things to us by His Spirit. As the Spirit of God meets with the spirit of man through worship, wisdom is transferred and revelation knowledge is received. Understanding, insight, perception of the Holy, and enlightenment literally flood the spirit of the true worshiper. A person benefits greatly from a true worship experience.

SHACHAH

What most of us recognize as worship is best described by the Hebrew term, *shachah*. It means "to worship Jehovah God, to bow down, to fall prostrate, to reverence and honor God with the words of our lips." With hymns and songs of worship, and with hands uplifted, or bowed knees, or prostrate, we adore and kiss the One that we love because of who He is. Worship says, You are our God strong and mighty in battle; our God full of tender mercies; our God who never forsakes us; our God who forgives all of our iniquities; our God who heals all of our diseases; our God who protects us from danger and evil; our God who forgets our past; our God who sees us through the eyes of compassion; our God who has promised to love us with an everlasting love in spite of who we are and what we have done.

To worship God with our words and an attitude of humility, with raised hands, kneeling, or lying prostrate, we are preparing ourselves for a deeper level of true worship. We may speak and sing in the spirit (in other languages), or in the understanding. When we have made a sacrifice of praise and worship, forsaking our needs and our own will, we sense the presence of God. His presence begins to heal our wounds, fill us with his power, give us a mind, and a mouth to speak wisdom with boldness. References made to an awesome God are the first words spoken by the true worshiper who has received a wisdom transfer.

Worship is a form of prayer, but it is on a much higher dimension. It is the highest form of prayer. Miracles can take place on any level that God desires to release them. However, in God's presence, miracles will always take place. Worship expresses the pure love of

God that He has placed in our hearts. Our worship reaches out to God in adoration, and returns His love back to Him. This love, we express in worship, moves God with compassion toward us extending an invitation to understand mysteries and secrets, and receive knowledge and wisdom. Because worship expresses pure love, there is no limit to what God will reveal. *Shachah* is one of the highest expression of our love in worship. This is the way we shower our God with blessings of our love and adoration.

THE PINNACLE OF WORSHIP

On a deeper and more intense level of true worship, worshipers are slain in the spirit. Falling to the ground on their faces as the presence of God fills the place, worshipers may lie prostrate for long periods of time. There is no need or ability to speak or stand. At the pinnacle of true worship, God speaks and ministers. The atmosphere is charged with God's presence, (the Shekinah). God speaks to us directly, through dreams, and in visions. Angelic messengers make visits to minister to the heirs of salvation. These messengers speak truth, impart wisdom, and reveal knowledge. The pinnacle of worship takes place only in an environment of honor, reverence, and the utmost respect for the only wise God. The worshiper is permitted entrance into the Holy of Holies. Once he is inside, there is no good thing that the Lord will withhold from him. Only true worshipers gain access to the Father's Most Holy Place. "Who shall ascend into the hill of the LORD? or who shall stand in his holy place? He that hath clean hands, and a pure heart; who hath not lifted up his soul unto vanity, nor sworn deceitfully. He shall receive the blessing from the LORD, and righteousness from the God of his salvation" (Ps. 24:3–5).

True worshipers have tried to explain their experiences, however their explanations just do not make sense to the natural man. True worship experiences are spiritually discerned. (See Daniel 8:15–18; Numbers 20:6–7; Genesis 17:1–3.) True worshipers have been criticized from the time men began to call on the name of the Lord.

In Exodus 7:16, we read that the Lord told Pharaoh to, "Let my people go, that they may serve me." The Hebrew word for serve is *abad*. It means worshiper. God was speaking words of wisdom to the pharaoh, but he was void of understanding. These words said, Pharaoh, I desire to save your life, if you will hear Me for just a moment. Pharaoh continued to move forward in his ignorance, which ultimately led to his death and the death of hundreds of thousands of others. The primary reason God sets people free from the slavery and bondage of sin is so they can worship Him. Do not waste time looking for wisdom in eloquent words. It will not necessarily be found there. It hides quite often in simple, common sense vernacular. Spend that time in worship.

CHAPTER 12

Worship Signifies That God
Has Fulfilled His Promise

A GREAT ARMY OF Moabites, Ammonites, and the children of Mt. Seir had come together to fight against King Jehoshaphat, Judah, and Jerusalem. The king decided to seek the Lord and proclaim a fast throughout all of Judah. He prayed before the Lord and poured out his heart unto God. All the cities of Judah began to seek the Lord. The Spirit of the Lord came upon the prophet Jahaziel, who gave the king and the people the following word of prophecy, "You will not need to fight, but set yourselves, and stand still and see the salvation of the Lord." When this word was spoken, "Jehoshaphat bowed his head with his face to the ground," (in an attitude of humility in worship). "And all Judah and the inhabitants of Jerusalem fell before the Lord, worshiping Him. And the Levites of the children of the Kohathites and the Korhites stood up to praise the Lord God of Israel with a loud voice." (See 2 Chronicles 17–19.)

Jehoshaphat and the inhabitants of Judah and Jerusalem worshiped the Lord. Then, the Levites broke forth in loud praises to the Lord. The armies of Israel had not fought or won any battle when they began to shout before the Lord in triumphant, victorious praise and worship. They had merely received a word of wisdom from God spoken though a prophet. But, when they heard the word of wisdom spoken, they began to send forth tumultuous praise and worship to their God. The king had already worshiped God, declaring how He had delivered Israel from its enemies in times past. The king worshiped God and said, in essence, "I know that you will deliver us out of trouble, again."

The next morning, they rose early and went to the place they had been instructed to go. And Jehoshaphat stood and encouraged the people, saying, "Believe in the Lord your God and ye shall be established; believe his prophets, so shall ye prosper" (2 Chron. 20:20).

But Jehoshaphat did not stop there. He continued in an attitude of praise and worship and appointed praise singers to praise the beauty of holiness as they went out before the army of their enemies. And they said, "Praise the Lord for His mercy endureth forever" (2 Chron. 20:21). And when they began to sing songs of deliverance, to praise and worship, the Lord ambushed Moab, Ammon, and Mt. Seir, and they turned against each other until all of them were utterly destroyed.

Judah and Jerusalem's praise and worship said to the Lord, "You have performed Your Word, Lord; Your promises are true. We have reigned triumphantly and victoriously over our enemies, and yet, we have not fought in this battle." Praise and worship moved Jehoshphat and the people from a position of fear to an attitude of faith, boldness, and trust in God. The word of wisdom came through the prophet only after King Jehoshaphat had worshiped the Lord and asked for wisdom regarding hostile armies. He stated that he did not know what to do, but he trusted the Lord to rescue them and their children from their enemies.

WORSHIP CREATES AN ENVIRONMENT CHARGED WITH THE FAITH THAT PRODUCES MIRACLES

The Syrophoenician

Matthew 15 includes the story of a woman from Canaan. She had come looking for Jesus, hoping that He would have compassion for her little girl who was demon-possessed. When she found Him, she said, "Have mercy on me, O Lord, thou Son of David; my daughter is grievously vexed with a devil" (Matt. 15:22). She wanted Jesus to heal her daughter and set her free from the power of the devil, but He refused to honor her request. The Lord told her, in essence, that healing and deliverance were for the children of God, not for dogs. He said that He would not take the children's bread (healing) and give it to her.

Mark describes this woman as a Greek, specifically from Syrophoenicia, which was the area of Tyre and Sidon in Biblical times. Today, this area is Lebanon. The Syrophoenicians worshiped Baal and the goddess Ashtaroth. Jezebel was the daughter of the King of Sidon. These people caused their children to pass through the fire, and they sacrificed them from the high places to these gods. (See Mark 7:25–26.)

When I was in Guatemala, I went to a Mayan Indian ruin that had become a tourist attraction and a national park. I saw the high places similar to ones referred to in the Scriptures. These places of human sacrifice were an abomination to the Lord. From the high places of ancient Sidon, Baal worshipers practiced human sacrifice. The steps up to the landing of the high place in Guatemala were numerous, and the high place was as tall as a three-story building. The Baal worshipers would carry their sacrifice up to the top of the high place and offer it Baal. Then, they would push the person down the stone steps. The way in which the steps were designed made it impossible for someone to stop themselves from rolling because they could not see the next step. When they reached the bottom, they were burned.

Some of the people on our trip climbed to the top of the Mayan high place. When they got ready to come down, they were afraid because of the way the steps were made. They had to sit down and come down each step one at a time and very slowly, because the succeeding step was designed in such a way that it went backward instead of forward. The people could not see the next step as they were coming down, and it was difficult for them to find it as they searched for it with one foot forward to guide them down safely from the high place.

When I considered the Syrophoenician's family background, I understood why the Lord had given her such a strong word of rebuke. She also understood why she was rebuked. The Lord was making reference to the Baal worship of the Syrophoenician people. His word of rebuke was really a question about her identification. In other words, He was saying to her, "Daughter, whose side are you on, the side of Baal, or the side of the Lord?"

Name-calling was not the issue. The doctrine of devil worship, witchcraft, sorcery, and all manner of the occult practiced by the Syrophoenicians was the focus of the Lord's rebuke. He was speaking to her about her spiritual life. I believe she was familiar with His voice and knew that He was a man of compassion because she had observed Him as He had healed others. She was not offended by His words. She knew He spoke the truth.

When Jesus refused to help the woman of Canaan she did not give up. She continued to make her request known unto the Lord even when the disciples asked Him to send her away. I can imagine the mockers, now incited by the attitude, and the comments of the disciples, saying, "Yea! Take that Canaanite woman and her lunatic daughter away from here." At that point she could have left in bitterness, but wisdom told her not to leave her post. Instead of walking away, she began to worship God.

Her godly worship made a powerful statement all by itself. It said, mama and daddy may have been devil worshipers, and grandpa and grandma may have been devil worshipers, but I am a worshiper of the true and living God. The King of glory is the focus of my worship and adoration. She proved beyond a shadow of doubt that she was not a Baal worshiper. She did not get angry when Jesus rebuked and refused her. She persevered because she had heard about the reputation of Jesus Christ, and she had come for her miracle. She continued to worship Him. Still, she was refused. But her worship had made her strong.

I believe that the woman from Canaan had spent time in worship that day before she came to Jesus. She came to Him with an attitude of worship. Her worship ushered her into a position of boldness and favor with God, and created an atmosphere charged with faith to produce a miracle. Imagine listening to her powerful words. Can you hear her calm, confident voice saying, "Truth, Lord: yet the dogs eat of the crumbs which fall from their master's table" (Matt. 15:27).

Worship will give you supernatural confidence that what you are doing is good and right. Her words may not seem like great words of wisdom, but the One who judges all things (and looks at the heart of an individual to discern the intents and purposes of the heart), thought that her words were great. These words are what I call a wisdom power pack. By wisdom, she made her declaration of faith and power. These famous words made a very strong pre-miracle statement. Her statement reaffirmed her conviction that her daughter would be made whole that day. Jesus confirmed and agreed with her, and told her that because of her faith, her dream would come true—and it did. Her daughter was healed in the same hour. These simple words, "Truth, Lord: yet the dogs eat of the crumbs which fall from their master's table," were some of the most profound words ever recorded in the history of mankind.

When she called Him Lord, she may have been repeating what she had heard someone else say. When she worshiped Him, she may have been imitating what she had seen someone else do, but as she worshiped, the spirit of the Lord began to transform her life. This transformation caused her to worship for real.

From the time of the earthly ministry of Jesus until today, the story of this woman has been told. The Canaanite woman's words placed her in the "Faith Hall of Fame." She is one of only two people referred to in the Scriptures as a person of "great faith" (Matt. 15:28). Everyone who has faith is, of course, flourishing in wisdom.

If you have a daughter or a son who is in trouble, follow the example set by this wise woman from Canaan. Here is what she did in three easy steps:

Step 1. She worshiped God.
Step 2. She asked the Lord to heal her child.
Step 3. Then, by faith, she declared her wisdom statement.

Here is a final note about the far-reaching, adverse, and lasting impact of Baal worship. Some historians have stated that the first people to discover and settle Britain were the Syrophoenicians. Today, in England, the church is struggling to survive while there is a resurgence of witchcraft and occult practices.

ABRAHAM

Abraham took his only begotten covenant child to become the sacrificial lamb in the land of Moriah. But Abraham declared in his wisdom statement that he and his son were going up into the mountain to worship. Even though his son was a dead man, so to speak, he worshiped the true and living God. Even as his child was lying on his deathbed, Abraham worshiped. When his son was about to leave this earth, he worshiped. His worship increased his faith and boldness as he told the child with words of wisdom, "the Lord will provide Himself a lamb" (Gen. 22:8). To me, these are also some of the most profound words of wisdom I have ever read. The power and glory of these words are found in their simplicity. And the Lord Jehovah Jireh did provide. The ram that was caught in the bushes by its horns became the sacrificial lamb for the burnt offering that day.

THREE WISE MEN

The ungodly understand the importance of worship. They know how to worship God better than some of us who are called the children of God. In Matthew 2:1–2, we read an unusual story of three wise men from the east who had seen the star of the One who was to be King of the Jews. The wise men had come to worship the King. Do you see the divine connection between wisdom and worship, yet? Wise men know how to worship God. I understand completely why God gives wisdom to the children of this world. This story is so significant because these three men were stargazers, astrologers, and prognosticators who received revelation knowledge directly from God regarding the Star of stars. In fact, they received so much enlightenment and insight about who Christ was, and the significance of His birth, that they left their stargazing and astrological businesses to bring gifts to the young King and worship Him instead of the stars. These men very likely made a lot of money doing what they did. The gifts they purchased for the King testifies to the tremendous insight they had gained about His identity. Gold signified His royalty. Frankincense represented the great High Priest, Christ, whose prayers are a sweet savor unto God. Myrrh is a spice that was used to prepare the Lord's body for burial. It testifies of the sacrificial Lamb of God.

The Spirit of God did not leave these men after they had seen the King, fallen down on their faces, worshiped Him, and presented Him with extravagant gifts. God continued to speak to the wise men who recognized and obeyed His voice. God spoke to them in a dream warning them not to go back to Herod. They obeyed God and took another route back home. The Lord trusted these men. They were so open-minded and teachable. These men had excellent spirits and the ability to receive information from God in a variety of ways. God had a plan of salvation for these three. He knew they loved wisdom so He showed them how to distinguish the real thing from the counterfeit. He knew they loved watching the stars so He directed them by what they thought was a star to the Daystar. Their lives were changed forever. When they returned home, I am sure that they continued to worship the King. As they did, they were led to honorable professions. I believe they never longed for their former lifestyle after their encounter with the King of kings. They became new creations in Christ. Their children's children are still worshiping the Bright and Morning Star, even unto this day.

Where there is wisdom, worship is present. Where there is worship, wisdom will soon make its way to that environment. In the midst of it all, there is faith to become the sons and daughters of God.

ON THE WAY TO THE BAHAMAS

I was on my way to the Bahamas one summer with four students. We had a two and a half hour layover in Miami. We relaxed and ate as we waited to board our next plane. About twenty minutes before boarding, I decided to check in with the airline agent to make sure everything was in order. We had been told at our departing airport, after our credentials had been checked, that we were confirmed all the way to Nassau and that we did not need to do anything but board our planes. At the counter in Florida, the agent asked for ID. One student had an uncertified birth certificate. I was aware of this when we left Michigan, but the agent who checked the ID told me that everything was in order.

Now, we are in Florida and it is twenty minutes before departure for Nassau. The agent who is preparing our boarding passes says the one student cannot continue with us, and that he will have to stay behind and be sent back to Michigan. I asked her if there were any alternative measures possible. She said there was nothing she could do, and that he would have to go back to Michigan. I assured her that he was the person his birth certificate said he was. I asked if she could give him his boarding pass and let him get on the plane. "Absolutely not," she said, "and even if I did, the authorities would detain him at the airport in Nassau and send him back." As I continued to talk with her about possible solutions, every suggestion I made and every question I asked received a negative response. I was praying and worshiping God as I had this encounter. I was up against a brick wall supported by tons of steel. Time was passing! I knew we needed divine intervention. Then, out of nowhere, another agent with more authority appeared. She was dressed in a beautiful pink suit. The other agents were dressed in navy blue or black. She asked the attending agent what the problem was. After their discussion, she looked at me as she spoke in a very professional and authoritative manner like an army general. In a very supportive way she said, "We have a bank in this airport that certifies birth certificates. It will cost five dollars, but you will not have time to get it done before the plane leaves." I asked her where the bank was. She told me where the bank was located. "It's where?" I asked. She repeated the location and the directions. Well, the student and I left to go to the bank. I stopped looking at my watch. There were only moments left before we were to board our plane and leave for Nassau. We went halfway across Terminal C to the down escalator. On the first floor of Terminal C we waited for a bus to take us from Terminal C to Terminal B. The bus seemed to take a lifetime before finally arriving. We boarded with other passengers who were going to Terminal B. We arrived and exited the bus, hastily. We entered Terminal B and hurried up the escalator to find the bank. We had to ask a couple of people for the location before we found it. Inside the bank the officer was friendly and helpful. We quickly told her our story in abbreviated, *Cliff Notes* form. She worked just as quickly to solve the problem, as she understood our dilemma. She swore him in, had him sign his birth certificate, and then sealed and certified his signature. We thanked her and paid the fee. Hurrying out of the bank, we easily found the down the escalator. On the first floor of Terminal B we waited at the bus stop. The bus came, we got on, and returned to Terminal C. When we got back to our departure gate, to my surprise, no one had boarded the plane. The agent who wanted to send the student back home greeted us with a smile. She did not seem to recognize us. Her demeanor and behavior were very routine. We gave her his birth certificate. She scrutinized it and gave us his boarding pass. She acted as if she was not aware that a miracle had just taken place. We even had time to sit down and relax before we were called to board our plane to Nassau. We were told that the plane was on time. We left Miami according to schedule. There was no delay in our departure. Time had stood still!

This was a situation in which God had to send a deliverer with words of wisdom. He had to go outside the camp, so to speak, and bring someone in who exercised wisdom, knowledge, and understanding. When a person is in deep trouble such as we were, it is disconcerting to deal with a fool, someone who is not knowledgeable, or unwilling to help. Paul asked the Thessalonians to pray for him so that God would deliver him from unreasonable and wicked men. God delivered us at the right time from one of the most unreasonable individuals I have ever encountered. I praise God that He has released wisdom into the earth. He will cause wisdom to work on your behalf through another person. Coming directly or indirectly to help you, wisdom will find its way to you if you will worship God. Through this ordeal, my spirit was singing songs of deliverance and praise.

YOU WILL BE HATED BECAUSE OF YOUR WORSHIP

People will hate you for your worship. Accept It. However, you must accelerate and increase in worship. Do not draw back. God is the focus of worship. So, go full speed ahead, worship and adore the King of glory. "Who is this King of glory? The LORD strong and mighty, the LORD mighty in battle" (Ps. 24:8).

King David danced before the Lord with all his might in worship. He had just brought the ark of God into the city with joy and gladness, shouting and the blowing of trumpets. There was a great celebration like no other, and the people rejoiced before the

Lord with King David. But David's wife Michal, Saul's daughter, did not celebrate the return of God's presence into the camp of Israel. She was not a participant in this glorious occasion. She despised David in her heart. She put him down and criticized him on the day that all Israel rejoiced because the ark of the Lord was returned into the city of David. She tried to make him look like a fool in his own eyes. The Hebrew word for *despise* is *bazah*, and it means "to condemn, to be scornful toward, or to consider a person to be vile or evil."

When one despises and criticizes the worshiper, that person sows seeds of destruction into his or her own life. They will never bear fruit, or give birth to their dreams. Their words can produce negative circumstances from which they never recover—until they repent.

Saul's daughter was a product of her father who had lost the kingdom. In spite of her heritage, God had given her the opportunity to restore credibility and respect to her father's name and memory. She missed a wonderful and unique opportunity. She was the queen of Israel, but she would not release the past so that God could bless her in the future. She was not happy when the ark of God (which represented God's divine presence) was brought into Jerusalem. She did not rejoice with her husband or the people over whom she reigned with her husband. She should have been overjoyed, but she was not happy with God's presence and she detested David because he was beside himself with joy as He praised and worshiped the Lord. Until the day of her death, Michal, King David's wife, never conceived or gave birth. Most women love to bear children, nurture them, and watch them grow in grace and in the admonition of the Lord.

CHAPTER 13

Bezaleel

THE BIBLE RECORDS the story of one individual who was exceedingly blessed with wisdom. As a descendant of the tribe of Judah, it can safely be concluded that he was a worshiper. I believe that he was selected to build the tabernacle of meeting because of his worship, not because he was gifted and talented. God had filled Bezaleel with His glory. When God spoke to Moses regarding the specifications for building the tabernacle, He also spoke to him about this man Bezaleel who would do the work:

> And the LORD spake unto Moses, saying, see, I have called by name Bezaleel the son of Uri, the son of Hur, of the tribe of Judah: and I have filled him with the spirit of God, in wisdom, and in understanding, and in knowledge, and in all manner of workmanship, to devise cunning works, to work in gold, and in silver, and in brass, and in cutting of stones, to set them, and in carving of timber, to work in all manner of workmanship. And, behold, I have given with him Aholiab, the son of Ahisamach, of the tribe of Dan: and in the hearts of all that are wise hearted I have put wisdom, that they may make all that I have commanded thee.
>
> —EXODUS 31: 1–6

What an anointing God had given Bezaleel. He was a multi-talented leader and a master builder. He would direct the workers to build the tabernacle according to God's commandment. From this we understand that God was extremely pleased with his life and the way in which he conducted himself in business. It was not Bezaleel's skill or ability that got God's attention. It was his fellowship in worship and prayer that placed the mantle of leadership upon his life. Bezaleel was clothed with wisdom. Those who would work with him also exercised wisdom and conducted their lives in a godly manner. Therefore, God gave them more wisdom. God said that He had put wisdom in the hearts of those who were already wise-hearted.

Not only was Bezaleel filled with the spirit of God in wisdom, understanding, and knowledge, he was gifted and talented in the fine arts. He had ability, skill, and intellect to work with silver, gold, and brass. He was a scholar, teacher, and mentor training those who worked with him to build the tabernacle. He personally made the most sacred, glorious, and important artifact in all history, the ark of the covenant. He handled the construction of the ark from beginning to end. He not only consulted with Moses, but he consulted with God through worship and prayer. Only those chosen and ordained by God to work in the office of a priest could touch or handle the ark. Those who were unauthorized to touch the ark of God would surely die. "And when they came to Nachon's threshingfloor, Uzzah put forth his hand to the ark of God, and took hold of it; for the oxen shook it. And the anger of the LORD was kindled against Uzzah; and God smote him there for his error; and there he died by the ark of God" (2 Sam. 6:6–7).

There is no doubt that the Spirit of excellence was upon Bezaleel's life. He was given the authority of God as he constructed not only the ark of the covenant, but also the tabernacle. Moses received the blueprint, but Bazealeel would bring the blueprint to life. How did he receive this anointing that was upon his life and in his heart?

CHAPTER 14

Worship and Wealth:
King Solomon's Life

KING SOLOMON'S LIFE gives us more insight into the kind of person that God blesses with wisdom. As we look at Solomon's character we see a type of Christ, one on whom and in whom God bestowed wisdom and wealth beyond an ordinary measure. I believe Solomon's wisdom was the manifestation of supernatural ability given to a mortal man. He is and will forever be the greatest wisdom and wealth expert the world has ever known. His most outstanding characteristic was integrity. He never prayed or asked God for money, riches, or wealth. The Scriptures give the following account about the man, Solomon:

> Behold, I have done according to thy words: lo, I have given thee a wise and an understanding heart; so that there was none like thee before thee, neither after thee shall any arise like unto thee. And I have also given thee that which thou hast not asked, both riches, and honour: so that there shall not be any among the kings like unto thee all thy days.
>
> —1 KINGS 3:12–13

85

> And God gave Solomon wisdom and understanding exceeding much, and largeness of heart, even as the sand that is on the sea shore. And Solomon's wisdom excelled the wisdom of all the children of the east country, and all the wisdom of Egypt. For he was wiser than all men; than Ethan the Ezrahite, and Heman, and Chalcol, and Darda, the sons of Mahol: and his fame was in all nations round about. And he spake three thousand proverbs: and his songs were a thousand and five.
>
> —I KINGS 4:29–32

As we determine what qualities Solomon possessed in order to receive these spiritual gifts (wisdom, honor, and wealth), we can safely assume that Bezaleel also had many of these attributes. Both Solomon and Bezaleel were chosen from the tribe of Judah. As a result, we know they were taught to praise and worship God from early childhood. Both were builders. They built houses in which God almighty would dwell. Let's examine Solomon's character more closely, for he was ordained to spread godly wisdom to the ends of the earth. He was also ordained to reveal the greatest wisdom secret for acquiring wealth, riches, and honor. This wisdom secret is simple: worship God and seek wisdom.

1. Solomon was a worshiper. In Gibeon, King Solomon sacrificed and offered one thousand burnt offerings before the Lord. At another time, He and all Israel offered unto the Lord 22,000 oxen and 120,000 sheep at the dedication of the temple. At another time, Solomon assembled all the congregation of Israel in Jerusalem and sacrificed such a great number of oxen and sheep they could not be counted. (See 1 Kings 3:4; 8:5, 62–63.) Under the old covenant, animal sacrifice was the highest form of worship. Solomon offered worship and led the people in worship before the Lord continually. Worship and adoration was proof of Solomon's life of dedication to the Lord.

2. He was an obedient son. King David not only taught his son the importance of worship, but how to worship.

David was a very wise man. He established the Levites to be praise and worship leaders before the Lord, in the tabernacle twenty-four hours a day. He was called the anointed of the God of Jacob, the sweet psalmist of Israel, the apple of God's eye.

King Solomon inherited an enormously wealthy estate from his father, King David. Yet, Solomon exceeded his father in wealth and wisdom writing three thousand proverbs and one thousand and five psalms of praise and worship. All the world sought Solomon to hear the wisdom which God had put in his heart. Kings and queens gave him gifts in exchange for wisdom on various topics and issues. He exceeded all the kings of the earth in riches and wisdom. Solomon was bestowed with the great honor of building the temple of God, an honor his father David greatly desired. Solomon had a teachable spirit and followed his father David's instructions and example. He accepted and received the legacy which his father David left him.

3. When Solomon asked God for wisdom, he asked for the right thing. His intentions were also right. He asked for wisdom and an understanding heart to judge the people righteously and to discern between good and evil. James 1:5 says, "if any of you lacks wisdom, he should ask God," the wisdom Giver to give him wisdom. When we ask God for anything, our motives for what we are asking must be right in the sight of God. And when we ask according to God's will, He will give freely and liberally without faultfinding or reproach. Here, we see the third prerequisite for receiving wisdom: asking according to God's will. God spoke to Solomon and said, "Ask me what shall I give you?" Solomon's response was an understanding heart.

4. The request for an understanding heart pleased the Lord. The fourth prerequisite for receiving wisdom is pleasing the Lord. The things we do in ministry and life must be pleasing to God. First Thessalonians 4:1

says that you ought to please God so that you can flourish more and more in the Kingdom of God. If we please the Lord, we are worthy of His blessings. His blessings bring increase in wisdom and knowledge. Sorrow is not added to our lives; instead God gives us gladness and joy.

5. During Solomon's request, he said these words to the Lord, "You have made your servant king," and, "I am but a little child" (1 Kings 3:7). Here is a man who has inherited extraordinary wealth and substance as well as the throne from his father, and is now king over Judah and Israel, a people who were as numerous as the sand by the sea. Solomon's kingdom was very vast, extending from the Euphrates river all the way to Egypt. Yet he humbled himself before the Lord, saying, "I am as a little child in the sight of God. I do not even know how to go out or come in" (1 Kings 3:7). Solomon had the common sense and knowledge to recognize that God was the source of his blessings—not his father David, not himself, but God and God alone—was the source. The fifth prerequisite for receiving wisdom is humility. A haughty spirit will never receive wisdom from God. The haughty spirit causes individuals to fall from grace, losing their positions in business, ministry, society, and so on. It makes a person think he or she knows everything, has everything, and is everything when, in reality, he or she is very, very needy. The Laodicean church had this spirit, "I am rich, and increased with goods and have need of nothing" (Rev. 3:17). But John said to these church members, "[you] knowest not that [you] art wretched, and miserable, and poor, and blind, and naked" (Rev. 3:17). This was a very strong rebuke, yet it was necessary to help the believers get a realistic view of their haughty attitudes, ungodly dispositions, and character. Proverbs 16:18 says, "Pride goeth before destruction, and an haughty spirit before a fall." Proverbs 11:2 says, "When pride cometh, then cometh shame: but with the lowly is wisdom." Wisdom is with the humble.

6. In 1 Kings 3:11–12, we read a statement that God spoke to Solomon, "Because thou hast asked this thing, and hast not asked for thyself long life; neither hast asked riches for thyself, nor hast asked the life of thine enemies; but hast asked for thyself understanding to discern judgment…I have given thee a wise and an understanding heart." The sixth prerequisite for receiving the gift of wisdom is selflessness. God told Solomon that there was no man who could compare to him in wisdom who had lived before him, and that no man would rise to the level of his greatness during his lifetime. God also told him that no man would ever be born who would exceed him in wisdom. "Solomon's wisdom exceeded" that of all wise men of the east and those of Egypt. His fame was in all of the nations. All the kings of the earth who had heard of his wisdom came to glean from him, and hear the words that God had given him. (See 1 Kings 4:29–34.) God also gave him two additional things which he never asked for—riches and honor. No king would ever exceed Solomon in riches or honor. None would be like him all the days of his life. Solomon had peace during his reign, and all the kings brought him presents every year and served him freely all the days of his life. Solomon's desire was for people to be wise. His unselfish attitude prompted God to bestow wisdom, knowledge, understanding, riches, wealth, and honor upon him. Some commentary writers and speakers have chosen to focus on Solomon's faults. However, until the critics surpass him in wisdom, and surpass him in riches, wealth, and honor, I will continue to glean from King Solomon, the ultimate expert on wisdom. Solomon was chosen and ordained to leave the whole world a legacy of godly wisdom. He fulfilled his mission. The only expert who surpasses him is the Lord Jesus Christ. The Lord is and always will be the only One who is without sin.

7. Solomon was a righteous judge. When there was a dispute among the people of his kingdom, he judged each case individually and justly. The people did not worry whether they would be treated fairly when they came before Solomon to settle a dispute. He judged without partiality, and the people trusted him.

8. Solomon was man of prayer. At one time when Solomon had finished praying, fire came down from heaven and consumed the burnt offering and the sacrifice he had made unto the Lord. The glory of the Lord filled the temple. The priests could not minister because the presence of God was so powerful, but under the same circumstances, Solomon was allowed to speak. King David served in the offices of both king and priest, and so did his son, Solomon.

9. "Solomon loved the LORD" (1 Kings 3:3). He walked in the ways of his father David. After a great sacrifice that Solomon made at Gibeon, the Lord appeared to Solomon in a dream and said, "Ask what I shall give thee?" (1 Kings 3:5). Solomon spoke to the Lord and all that he asked of Him during his dream became a reality.

10. Solomon was a dreamer. It is ordained of God for us to dream, because without a vision we will perish. Dreams and visions come from God. Some dreams and visions warn us of impending danger, others are prophetic in nature. Some dreams speak to us about the present. God spoke to Solomon in a dream. Solomon answered the Lord during the same dream. It was not until he woke up that he realized he had been communing with God in a dream. When men say that things are impossible, God says that those same things are very possible. He will speak to you about His plan for your life in a dream or in a vision late at night, when you are in a deep sleep. This is the time when God will open your spiritual understanding and cause

you to hear His words. And He will give you instructions to follow and seal the vision, so that it will not
fail, but will come to pass according to the right time
and season. (See Job 33:14–16.)

11. From the time Solomon was born, there was spiritual
    quality in his character and nature that made God
    love him. "The LORD loved" Solomon. (See 2 Samuel
    12:24.) This Scripture also applies to us, because God
    so loved the world that he gave His only begotten Son
    to die for our sins. When we accept the Son as Savior,
    we receive eternal life. God sees in every human being
    spiritual quality that transcends what we can com-
    prehend through our senses or intellect. This spiritual
    quality is what makes us God's beloved.

12. A true worshiper is a master builder. Both Bezaleel
    and Solomon were master builders. These two wor-
    shipers built spiritual houses so that God could dwell
    among His people. God called Bezaleel to build the
    tabernacle. He called Solomon to build the Temple.
    Both of these buildings represented spiritual houses,
    which were types and shadows of things to come.
    They were examples to let us know that God's desire
    to live among His people is very real. This is God's
    heart's desire.

13. Bezaleel and Solomon were men of peace, not war.
    True worshipers are men of peace. Those who caused
    bloodshed in times of war were not asked to build the
    house of God. It is the blood the sacrificial Lamb of
    God that makes the atonement for sin, not the blood-
    shed of war.

14. God could trust these two men of integrity. He
    would not have chosen them to be recipients of His
    miraculous power if they were untrustworthy, double
    minded, and tossed by every wind of doctrine. They
    were not men of excuses. They did not complain about

the complexity of the work they had to do. They both completed their work with joy and gladness. They considered it a great honor indeed to be trusted and chosen to do God's work.

These qualities found in the heart of a true worshiper moves God to a place of compassion. God longs for us to fellowship and commune with Him in worship so that He can fulfill our needs and grant our desires. When God finds true worship, He pours out His Spirit in the earth and the true worshiper receives spiritual gifts. There is a divine connection between worship and wisdom that cannot be denied or broken. The eyes of the Lord run to and fro throughout the whole earth to show Himself strong on behalf of those whose hearts are perfect toward Him. (See 2 Chronicles 16:9.)

King Solomon was ordained to operate in a ministry that I call wisdom authority. It was a position of distinction and great magnitude. Yet, the beauty and splendor of his wisdom strategies are found in simplicity and common sense. Do you wish to move and minister in the office of wisdom? If the answer is yes, then keep it simple and exercise common sense.

Those who have made the divine connection between worship and wisdom are the individuals who will receive wisdom, wealth, riches, and honor, both in this world and in that which is to come. As God looks throughout the earth to find those upon whom He will bestow these gifts, He is looking for the qualities of the true worshiper. King Solomon and Bezaleel were true worshipers. They had been raised in an environment of worship. As adults, however, they had the choice to walk away from the teachings of their parents, or walk in the ways of their parents. They could have used their wealth for corruption, but they chose to keep covenant with the God of their fathers.

It is never too late or early to become a worshiper. Age should not be used as an excuse. Just get on your knees and tell God whatever is on your mind. Give Him testimonies and praise. Tell Him your troubles. Pour out your heart. In the best way that you know how, worship the King.

Part III:

The World

For God so loved the world, that he gave his only begotten Son, that whosoever believeth in him should not perish, but have everlasting life.

—JOHN 3:16

CHAPTER 15

God Loves the World

N EVER DOUBT IT! God sent His Son into the world not to condemn, but to save. God has blessed the children of the world with wisdom so that He can draw them close to Him, and save them.

The Son of God has chosen disciples and given them power, the authority of His name, protection through His blood, the Holy Spirit, and surrounded us with His everlasting love for a divine purpose. God has filled us with His compassion and wisdom so that through our testimony the whole world could be saved. It is not God's will for any man to perish, but He desires for all to repent and be transformed into His image.

We must be an example, a living epistle to the sinner to help him turn from sin to righteousness, to teach him to seek and find the true, living, and only wise God. If, through wisdom, we are a living example of God's ambassadors of love and peace, the world will be reconciled to Christ. When we were God's enemies, and actively engaged in sin, God reconciled us to Himself through the death of His Son, Jesus Christ. Now He has given us a ministry of reconciliation so that we can have compassion for the lost.

God commanded His love to come to us while we were slaves to sin. He did not offer His love to us after we were saved and sanctified, but while we were still sinners, Christ died for us: And not just for us, but for all humanity He died. The world and those who dwell in it belong to God: And just as God was merciful, demonstrating His love for us, how much more should we show love and mercy to those who are lost?

A time is coming when, "All the ends of the world shall remember and turn unto the LORD: and all the kindreds of the nations shall worship before..." the King of kings and Lord of lords. (See Psalm 22:27.) I want to make sure that I play a major role in the turning of the nations unto the Lord. As I continue to worship God, He will give me wisdom strategies to use so that I can keep changing the world for His glory.

THE OUTPOURING

God has a wisdom plan to save the whole world. He continually pours out His Spirit upon the people of the earth in a very great measure. I believe we will see another extraordinary outpouring of the Spirit of God before the Lord returns. While the world is corrupt and the wickedness in the earth is great, God will signify the coming of the Lord by a marvelous sign:

> It shall come to pass in the last days, saith God, I will pour out my Spirit upon all flesh; and your sons and daughters, shall prophesy, and your young me shall see visions, and your old men shall dream dreams: And on My servants and handmaids, I will pour out in those days of My Spirit; and they shall prophesy.
>
> —ACTS 2:17–18

The great outpouring of God's Spirit will cleanse the earth from the bloodshed of many innocent people. It will usher in the coming of the Lord and touch old and young, male and female, everywhere. Entire cities, and even the majority of the people in some nations, will be transformed by the outpouring of God's Spirit. The world will see positive changes in the lives of individuals, in the economies of cities, and in the leadership of nations. Positive change in all aspects of a person's life will be evident. Wisdom will be seen in all a person does. Their health will be restored, wealth and honor will be in the person's house. Positive changes in hostile governments and their leaders will be a testimony of God's omnipotent power. The transformation will cause some to seek God, while others will seek after the material things, and others will mock and scoff, but none will be able to deny the power of God.

The outpouring will equip God's messengers. End-time apostles, prophets, pastors, evangelists, teachers, and ministers will teach, preach, prophesy, and evangelize the entire world. They will heal the sick, raise the dead, speak with new tongues, save souls, and walk in the wisdom of God. Every man, woman, and child will hear the Gospel and be touched by God's miraculous power.

IN TIMES OF INSTABILITY, WISDOM BRINGS STABILITY

"In the world ye shall have tribulation: but be of good cheer; I have overcome the world" (John 16:33). We live in times of great trouble, and there is instability. Certain events of our decade have changed the face and structure of the world forever. But we have the assurance that God knows the beginning from the end of all things. In the midst of every uncertainty, we know that "wisdom, knowledge, and strength of salvation will be the stability of our times" (Isa. 33:6). I believe that wisdom increases in times of instability. The need and ability for wise decision making arises out of instability. The God-given ability that is in the spirit of a wise-hearted person can cause God to turn the issues of life the enemy means for evil into something wonderful. This God-given ability is worship.

I remember a time when I needed to change jobs in order to restructure my status in a particular organization. I began to pray, seek the Lord, and worship Him. I knew I had to take a risk. I could not listen to those who were telling me that times were too unstable, and that what I was doing was too risky. They were right, under normal circumstances, it was risky. People told me to hold on, wait, stay put, make the move later. I had to withdraw myself from them, spiritually, and listen to the voice of wisdom. In my mind and emotions I was in agreement with what was being said to me, yet inside, I had such peace. With the odds against me, I left one position not knowing what the future would hold for me, but

I continued to worship and trust the Lord. I did not take a step of "blind faith," if there is any such thing. Wisdom directed me step by step. As it turned out, I was hired by another company with no loss of time between the two positions. I know that I am going to face even greater tests in the future. I am taking the necessary steps to prepare for these tests. I have decided that I am going to sail through them all as I worship the King of glory.

How will we remain steadfast and unmovable, always experiencing the love of God in times of instability, turmoil, and terror? The answer is through worship. As we worship, we will receive wisdom that will bring stability into our souls, our homes, our ministries, our cities, our schools, the workplace, the marketplace, our governments, and into nations.

THE WORLD NEEDS OUR PRAISE AND WORSHIP

True praise and worship of the righteous, as it is heard over the airwaves throughout the whole earth, has a profound and positive impact in the lives of those who are in the world. True worship also cancels the destructive work of demonic influence, which is released into the world through satanic music. Worship restores the soul and brings peace and clarity of insight. It creates an atmosphere in which a person can receive wisdom and knowledge from God. Wisdom is full of knowledge. God reveals His ideas that can bring stability into any situation. When a person's mind is stable, he or she has a heart that is ready to make a life-changing decision for Christ. We will never know the full extent to which godly worship is bringing hope and help to a lost generation, unless Jesus gives us insight into this matter. I believe that worship has affected the world in the same way that it affected King Saul when David played the harp and sang psalms. The Bible says that an evil spirit would come and trouble Saul. His servants sought David to come and play the harp when the evil spirit troubled the King. As David played songs of praise and worship, the evil spirit left and Saul was delivered, revived, and refreshed. When the world hears praise and worship from the heart of a true worshiper, they will be delivered from evil spirits. When praise and worship goes into all the world, deliverance and peace will come into the souls of many in these latter days. Many souls will hear and respond positively to wisdom's call of salvation. However, a distinct line of demarcation drawn in red, representing the blood of Jesus Christ, must separate godly praise and worship from its counterfeit.

I want to pray now and ask the Lord to perfect His praise and worship in you.

> *Father, in Jesus' name, perfect Your love in the reader. Give them a heart of worship, praise, thanksgiving, and gratitude toward You. Forgive them for lack of time spent in Your presence. Fulfill their desire to be filled with the Spirit of wisdom, revelation knowledge, understanding, skill, and ability. They desire an excellent spirit. They desire to redeem the time that has been lost in these evil days. As we speak to You, and sing about You in our praise and worship, may a heart be captured for Jesus Christ, forever. Amen.*

CHAPTER 16

Keep Yourself Unspotted From the World

SECOND PETER 1:4 says that God has given us, "great and precious promises: that by these ye might be partakers of the divine nature, having escaped the corruption that is in the world through lust." The world in which we live is very corrupt, and will someday pass away with its lusts. We have been delivered out of the world's corruption through Christ Jesus. We are in the world, but we are not of this world. The world is the place in which we give birth to our children and raise them. It is the place in which we work and engage in the activities of men.

Through Christ, we have received God's divine nature and, although we are in the world, we can live in the Kingdom of our God and of His Christ while we are on the earth. For it is in Christ that we live, move, and have our existence in this present world. We are challenged on every hand to become more and more like the world because we are in the world. However, we are not without the power of God, which is always available to us. Jesus said, "Behold, I give unto you power to tread on serpents and scorpions, and over all the power of the enemy: and nothing shall by any means hurt you" (Luke 10:19). Power is useless unless it is exerted. Exerted power enforces the will of God, bringing victory as we overcome the world.

We are in the world because of a divine plan which God ordained before the foundation of the world. That plan is for His glory to fill the whole earth through His body of believers. God's glory will not fill the earth through angelic beings, or worldly individuals, for there is no fellowship between light and darkness. The Lord has instructed us to go and make disciples in all nations, teaching them the Word of God and baptizing them in the name of the Father, the Son, and the Holy Spirit. When the Light of the glorious Gospel has been preached in all the world, the glory of the Lord shall fill the whole earth. The Light of His glory will shine through people from every nation, tribe, and tongue. When this happens, the end of all things will surely come, and the beginning of peace will be established.

When we exercise wisdom, the world will never captivate us with lying signs and wonders. We will never allow the world to conform us to its ways. But, we will shape and mold the history of the world for Jesus Christ. His glory should leave its trademark everywhere we go. God's trademark is His goodness. When we leave a place, God's goodness should be left behind.

WISDOM'S WARNING

The voice of wisdom has warned us, concerning the world:

1. Do not to be conformed to, or in agreement with, the systems of this world.

The god of this world has blinded the minds, and hidden the Gospel from, those who do not believe in the Lord Jesus Christ. We must not be like those who engage in all forms of wickedness, evil, and exploitation. We should be transformed, (not conformed) by renewing our minds through study of, and meditation on, God's Word. As a person meditates in the Word, wisdom will reveal Jesus Christ; unveil the perfect will of God; and give instructions for every situation, issue, dilemma, and problem one will ever face in life. The victory that overcomes the world is our faith in God who will give us wisdom secrets to use as we make the world a better place.

Joseph, the governor of Egypt, grew stronger in wisdom through great trials and tribulations. The Pharaoh spoke this concerning

Joseph. "Can we find such a one as this is, a man in whom the Spirit of God is…there is none so discreet and wise as [you are]" (Gen. 41:38–39). Joseph had opportunity to be conformed to the world in which he lived, but he refused to be a partaker in another man's sin.

2. Do not love the world, or the things that are in the world.

If anyone loves the world, the love of God is not in him. (See 1 John 2:15–16.) The following three things are all that the world has to offer:

A. The lust of the flesh
B. The lust of the eyes
C. The pride of life

None of these things come from God. They come from the god of this world, Satan. The world and its lusts are passing away, but those who obey God will abide forever. (See 1 John 2:17.)

In the presence of God is, "fulness of joy; at [His] right hand there are pleasures for evermore" (Ps. 16:11). Therefore, a righteous man will not find pleasure indulging in the lusts of the flesh and the eyes, or the pride of life. He seeks "pleasures for evermore." These eternal and everlasting pleasures are found in Christ. Worship will bring you into God's presence where pleasures dwell.

3. Do not keep worldly friendships.

James 4:4 says, "Know ye not that the friendship of the world is enmity with God? whosoever therefore will be a friend of the world is the enemy of God." Say goodbye to your worldly friendships. You can witness, testify, and pray for your worldly friends, but you cannot keep company with them. Release these companionships to the Lord. He has expertise in handling them. You must draw the line between worldly friendships and being God's friend. As God's friend, you can receive wisdom to help a friend convert to Christ.

If you are sleeping with the world, "Awake thou that sleepest, and arise from the dead, and Christ shall give thee light" (Eph. 5:14). He is the Light of the world. He will illuminate your path. He is the One who will show you how to live as one who is wise and not a fool. He alone can lead you into paths of righteousness and keep you firmly planted on the Rock of Salvation.

TRUE FRIENDSHIP

I was discussing true friendship with my daughter the other day. Her definition of *friend* was someone with whom you communicate and socialize. This was a good definition, but it was incomplete. At the end of our discussion, we came up with a good way of identifying "true friends."

Jesus sets the example. He was a single young man, a minister of righteousness, chosen by God for a unique purpose. He was tempted like we are, but He was without sin. Jesus carefully chose His friends. A true friend cannot just walk into your life. They must be chosen wisely, as the Lord did when choosing His followers. Choose your friends wisely, based on the Word of God, because the devil sends imposters into a person's life to overturn the plan of God.

The initial twelve apostles were men of character who were teachable and had leadership qualities. Because Jesus would have to work very closely with the apostles, women were not among the twelve chosen. The Bible says that we are not to have the appearance of evil. As a single man, the Lord did not have women as his traveling companions. The companions of singles of all ages should have high moral standards, outstanding character and behavior, and be of the same sex. This will help one avoid sexual temptation, keep one's mind focused on the Lord, and keep one clean both in body and spirit.

Jesus remained close to the disciples until His death. True friends stick closer than a brother. True friends will always draw you to Christ. They will not cause you to compromise your moral values to satisfy their selfish motives. True friends are selfless. Jesus laid down His life for His friends. They tell you the truth when you are wrong even if it means losing your friendship. They stick by you when others leave because of tragedy, misfortune, or hardship. A true friend tells you to stop doing what you are doing if it is wrong.

CHAPTER 17

The Last Days

Wisdom and knowledge shall be the stability of thy times.
—Isaiah 33:6

THE WORLD AND its systems have an underground network in place for the express purpose of invading, controlling, taking over, and finally destroying the body of Christ. This network seeks to lure our children into a web of evil perversion. But God's will is to fill them with His Spirit in wisdom, knowledge, understanding, skill, and ability in the arts, craftsmanship, and business. God's will is for them to live out their days in health and prosperity of the soul and spirit. Remember, many antichrists are already at work in the world. "For many deceivers are entered into the world, who confess not that Jesus Christ is come in the flesh. This is a deceiver and an antichrist" (2 John 7). And it is this spirit of deception that goes after our children, and after us, too. The enemy's assignment is to destroy God-given plans and dreams, to crush God ideas, squelch insight and creative thoughts. With the dregs of despair, the enemy covers hope and expectation of a successful and prosperous future. And when all hope is gone, the spirit of deception sends the spirit of death to hover over a person's life. Praying in the spirit will destroy the activity of this demonic power.

In These Last Days

One key element that we all recognize in identifying these last days is accelerated violence. The number of angry people in the world seems to have multiplied. We are surrounded by terror. There is no hiding place, except "under the blood" of Jesus Christ. Paul wrote to Timothy about the conditions of the world in the last days. He told Timothy that awful and terrible days would come. Paul said people within the nations of the world would be selfish, covetous, boastful, proud, blasphemers, disobedient to parents, unthankful, unholy, without natural affection, trucebreakers, false accusers, out of control, fierce, haters of God and good, traitors, greedy of gain, ever-learning but never really coming into the knowledge of truth or of God; snobbish, and loving pleasure more than they love God. They have a form of godliness, but in reality they deny the power of God. Silly women will be taken captive by this web of ungodliness. From such, turn, walk away, and do not look back. Do not take part in their sins. (See 2 Timothy 3:1–7.)

Who are these people and where are they? They are "everyday" people in your community, your city, and schools. They sit beside you every Sunday at church. They work in the public and private sector, in government, and they have businesses in the marketplace. Some are the ones that you least expect to fit Paul's description— friends and family members.

Matthew also wrote about the signs that would precede the Lord's return and the end of the world. He said that many false prophets would come and deceive many saying they were Christ. There would be wars and rumors of wars, nation would rise against nation. Believers would betray one another and hate one another. Many would be offended, and because of the greatness of sin on the earth, many would no longer walk in brotherly love. (See Matthew 24.)

However, the Lord prepared us for these last days in which we live. He laid down His life for the sins of the entire world. He saves those who believe on His name. He has given another Comforter, the Holy Spirit, "that He might deliver us from this present evil world, according to the will of God" (Gal. 1:4). As believers, we have been given powerful spiritual weapons of war: the blood, the name, power, our testimony, praise and worship, and the living Word, Himself. We have the full armour of God. We also have other weapons of war: our God who is an all consuming fire, the blast of the breath of His nostrils, the hammer of God, the new threshing instrument, and many others. After we have been converted and delivered, and given spiritual weapons of war, and are known by God as His holy people, should we turn again to the weak and beggarly elements of the world and be entangled again in bondage? (See Galatians 4:9.) Should we become slaves to this present darkness when we have access to the Father by one Spirit? We have free access to His Kingdom, and all that is in His treasury through Christ.

Paul wrote to the church in Corinthians concerning the lusts that are in the world, and how the forefathers were taken captive by the same lusts that exist today. He explained to them that God was not pleased with their behavior, and that their experiences were recorded as examples for us even today, so that we would not lust for evil as they did. Paul told the church not to be covetous as some of them were. He explained that the people sat down to eat and drink and rose up to play, and that twenty-three thousand fornicators died in one day. Some tempted Christ and were bitten by serpents. Some of them complained and were destroyed as the earth opened up and swallowed them. Paul said that we should not be like them. For we have been purchased out of the world by God for a great price, His only begotten Son. Christ has a predestined plan to secure victory over every temptation and test of the last days.

Will we allow the huge tidal wave of the last days issues to wash us away and separate us from the love of God? Or will we be responsible for delivering thousands of thousands out of their issues? When Paul wrote to the Romans, he tested them with a question, "Who shall separate us from the love of Christ? shall tribulation, or distress, or persecution, or famine, or nakedness, or peril, or sword? As it is written, For thy sake we are killed all the day long; we are accounted as sheep for the slaughter. Nay, in all these things we are more than conquerors through him that loved us. For I am persuaded, that neither death, nor life, nor angels, nor principalities, nor powers, nor things present, nor things to come, nor height, nor depth, nor any other creature, shall be able to separate us from the love of God, which is in Christ Jesus our Lord." (Rom. 8:35–39). Wisdom will preserve and keep you in your right mind through every test and temptation.

Isaiah wrote about the condition of the earth in the last days also, "For, behold, the darkness shall cover the earth, and gross darkness the people: but the LORD shall arise upon thee, and his glory shall be seen upon thee" (Isa. 60:2).

I am fully persuaded that the last days' darkness will not separate me from God's love. I believe that His glory which is upon my life contains all the necessary ingredients for me to rise far above this present darkness. I believe that in the light of His countenance is life and favor for me, and that His glory is forever present with answers to life's hard questions. The wisdom I desire, and the expectation and hope that my latter days will be greater than the former, is ever present with me and it can be the same with you, also.

MONEY, WEALTH, RICHES: DO NOT LOVE MONEY, FOR THE LOVE OF MONEY IS THE ROOT OF ALL EVIL

1 TIMOTHY 6:10

The Bible says the ungodly prosper in the world and increase in riches. The Psalmist Asaph was envious of the wicked and the foolish when he saw their prosperity. Much of their prosperity had been secured through the perversion network whether openly or covertly. It was very painful for Asaph to watch the way in which this network maneuvered against his generation. They were strong and did not die early. They were not in trouble or plagued with problems like other men. They were proud, violent, covetous, and had more than their heart could ever wish to have. They were greedy. But soon, God led Asaph into the sanctuary. There, he began to worship God and to pray. Suddenly, God opened the eyes of his understanding and gave him revelation knowledge regarding the destruction of the wicked. He received wisdom and insight, and as he saw their end he was no longer jealous of the wicked. (See Psalm 73.)

Never be envious of those who are prosperous based on the world's standards. We know that true riches come from God. One of the most valuable possessions a person can obtain is wisdom.

Financial prosperity is not an end. It is a means by which the Gospel will be spread to all nations, until it reaches from shore to shore, border to border, sea to sea. Wealth has a purpose. Its mission is to support the Gospel until it reaches the four corners of the earth, every nation, tongue, tribe, creed, and population on the face of the earth. The primary purpose of economic success is to feed the hungry, clothe the naked, house the poor, and heal the sick in the name of the Lord. Then, introduce the Savior and His Gospel to someone whose stomach is full, whose water is clean, and whose nakedness is covered. (See the story of the storage builder in Luke 12:16–21.)

People Who Are in Need Do Not Care About How Much Money You Have

Quite frankly, money will not fill anyone with joy. But when money feeds starving children, builds schools and orphanages, establishes clinics and hospitals, and provides clean drinking water and medical supplies to the needy, then money is talking. It is speaking the language of love and everyone understands its voice.

Helping the poor should be a top priority of the wisdom seeker. As you grow in wisdom, God will release the power for you to get wealth, and tell you how to use it for His glory. (See Deuteronomy 8:18; Ecclesiastes 5:19.) In Deuteronomy 15:11, the Bible says, the poor will never cease to exist in the earth. This statement is also recorded again in Matthew 26:11. The Lord instructs us to give abundantly and liberally to help the poor and needy. Therefore, make sure that you have money. You need it. Just do not let your money have you! If God cannot trust you with handling someone else's money or your own money, He will never trust you with true riches.

CHAPTER 18

Protected From Evil
in This Present World

Surely goodness and mercy shall follow me all the days of
my life.

—PSALM 23:6

IN THE DAY of adversity, no tragedy, no calamity, no plague, no
evil, or sudden destruction will come upon a righteous person.
There will always be a warning of impending danger, and a strategic plan of escape. The righteousness of the perfect will direct his
path. This means that because a righteous man seeks wisdom and
discretion, and he follows God's instructions, God will preserve and
keep him from the snare of the enemy in the day of trouble:

Now unto him that is able to keep you from falling, and to
present you faultless before the presence of his glory with
exceeding joy.

—JUDE 1:24

We do not have to fall into traps set by the god of this present
evil world, but if we fall seven times or more, we will arise, because
God will deliver and restore us from evil.

One day, I was conducting a prayer meeting when a young woman came into the prayer room. She was very distressed and troubled. She said, "I need someone to pray with me, I need to know what to do." This young woman was seeking godly wisdom. She had just graduated from Bible college. She and her fiancé, a minister, were going to be married in about two weeks. They were going into full-time ministry and start a church. Her fiancé worked for the women's state penitentiary system. During the three weeks before they were to be married, she learned that he had befriended a mentally retarded woman who was an inmate at the prison. She was serving time for a drug-related incident. The woman received a certain amount of money every month from a government agency and had no place to live upon her release from prison, according to the fiancé.

The fiancé took the inmate home to live with him upon her release from prison. He tried to get his fiancé not only to agree with what he was doing, but he asked her to move in with them after the wedding so that they could become a happy threesome. As I listened to this story, I was amazed that the man had almost succeeded in convincing the young woman to go along with his scheme.

The troubled young woman had even gone to the retarded woman asking her to leave her fiancé's apartment because their wedding day was quickly approaching. She pleaded with her fiancé to move the woman into an assisted living facility. She had prayed and cried asking God to correct the mess so that she could marry this man on their scheduled wedding date. She said to me, over and over again, "He should put her out, he should put her out. She should leave!" "I told her to get out. Don and I are going to be married in just a few days."

Okay! I said to the Lord, *So what if the 'other woman' does get out?* Getting the retarded woman out of the fiancé's apartment was not the central theme of the young Bible student's need. The fact that she had come for prayer regarding the matter was evidence to me that she loved the Lord and that He wanted to deliver her from evil. What she needed was:

1. A clear vision of the kind of person the fiancé really was.
2. A revelation of God's plan and purpose for her life.
3. To realize that she was in a test.

4. To decide whether she would choose life over death;
   and pass the test.

Well, to make a long story short, the evil one had come to completely destroy this young Bible college graduate's life through deception. She was at a crossroads. In a moment, she could step into a life of perversion, drugs, and violence, or she could repent and wholeheartedly return to the Lord. She could walk away from this whole mess and be set free by the Son who sets people free indeed. Or, she could accept the death sentence that was presented to her. She was distressed emotionally, but she was still able to make the right decision.

When she finished her story, I looked her squarely in the eyes and said, "Now unto Him who is able to keep you from falling" (into a mess that will increase in immorality, perversion, and evil work), and "present you blameless and faultless before the presence of His glory with exceeding joy, be glory and honor forever." (See Jude 1:24.)

"I am glad that you came into the prayer room today," I continued. "God will not allow you to fall, if you really want to serve Him. He will give you a specific plan of attack against the enemy. He will hide you in His secret place while you make your escape to safety. Run to Him and seek Him while He can be found. Never look back or regret how God delivered you this day out of the hand of the enemy."

Through wisdom, God keeps us from falling prey to Satan's evil and wicked schemes. He will also deliver the righteous man out of trouble, but God prefers to keep the righteous person from falling into trouble. This does not mean that the righteous will not have tribulations and tests. This Bible student had favor with God. She had taken two years of her life and set it aside as a time to study the Word, worship the Lord, and prepare herself before the Lord for ministry. The devil hated her immensely as he does all mankind and especially God's children. He had made his plan so appealing by telling her that she would get married to a minister, go into full-time ministry, and start a church, which was her heart's desire. This clouded her vision and she could not see the evil work.

The Bible says that the single person should keep his or her mind totally focused on the things of the Lord, learning to please Him.

As a result of keeping a God-centered life, the single individual will remain clean, pure, and holy both in body and spirit. This is an area in which the devil causes confusion in a person's life. If someone believes that he or she has been single long enough, they will begin to look for a mate, even if is not according to God's plan. This gives the devil an opportunity to introduce an imposter to the person. In the case of this young woman, God spared her life because she had made a sacrifice for two years and prepared herself for ministry. Although she had assumed that starting a church and working in ministry would have automatically eradicated the problem, and presented the opportunity for herself and her fiancé to live happily ever after, God protected her and delivered her from a death trap.

CONFERENCE IN INDIANAPOLIS

The outcome was not as positive for another young lady that we will call Janice. She had met a young man over the Internet and decided to go visit him at his college campus. Janice invited me and another friend to come to a conference in her city. I really did not want to go because I had just returned from our family reunion, and my budget for that month had been exhausted. I did not want to travel at that time, but she insisted that we come. Our mutual friend, another young woman that I had mentored, found one of those two for one flights. I begin to pray about the trip. I spoke with my husband. He said that I could go if I wanted to do so. I sensed that the Lord wanted me to go.

When we arrived in Indianapolis, Janice met us at the airport. She had a trailer and we stayed with her. After attending the conference for a day and a half, Janice begin to share the story about her new boyfriend. She was going to his college campus to meet him for the first time. She was happy and excited. I begin to question her about who he was, and caution her about going. I asked her where she would stay when she got to the campus. She continued to tell me about how she knew his sister, but she did not know much about him. She would stay with him in his dorm room when she got there. She asked me to agree with her about the trip to meet this young man and stay in his dorm room. She did not want prayer. She would not exercise wisdom. She did not want advice. She simply wanted agreement that it was the right thing to do. I prayed for her. I told her emphatically not to go, and that what she was doing was not the will of God. She went anyway. Putting it mildly, the whole episode, from beginning to end was a disaster.

TEEN QUEEN

A high school student wanted to participate in a national Teen Queen contest. She completed the application process and sent in her initial fees. Her parents were happy, as they proceeded with the endeavor, and made preparation for their daughter's entrance and success. The daughter was bright, talented, and beautiful. Her parents decided to fast and pray for three days concerning the matter to get the perfect will of God, and insight for their daughter's success. At the end of the first day of prayer, a red flag went up. The Lord revealed that the teenager would be stalked. The parents and the daughter went into prayer on the second day. Their focus was to bind demonic forces, release the will of God, and surround their daughter with divine protection. At the end of the second day, instead of getting the go ahead to proceed with the contest, another red flag went up. By this time, they learned that their daughter had received the official title representing her city and county in the contest. In prayer, they learned that one of the officials in the contest organization preyed on young girls. This was the second red flag. The parents were beginning to sense that the Teen Queen contest was not something in which their daughter should participate. They were anticipating a confirmation from God, that the "stalker" had been bound and that it would be safe for their daughter to continue in the contest, instead, they got another word of caution.

They were praying on the third day. The word of wisdom spoke now a third time. It was another red flag. At the end of prayer, the mother began to question her daughter about the use of the Internet. She had parental blocks on the computer and had not given any of her children permission to use it without supervision. The daughter admitted to chatting with strangers over the net. The mother continued to question her, asking if she had ever sent a picture of herself to anyone with whom she had chatted. The daughter's answer was, yes. In an instant, the parents received full revelation knowledge concerning the third red flag. As a contestant, the daughter would be a public figure, on the local, state, and national levels. Her life would no longer be private. Once the news about her being a contestant hit the media, her life would be open to media scrutiny. The person with whom she had chatted over the Internet could have seen her in the news. He could have done any number of things with the picture she had sent. He also would have learned in what community, city, and state she lived. That was the end of the contest for this young lady. Wisdom will not necessarily be a bearer of good news in the form that you are expecting it, but wisdom will always be a bearer and speaker of the truth. In essence, the truth is good news.

RIGHTEOUSNESS

The term "righteous person" means someone who is born of God and who is living a clean and holy life based on God's commandments. The person is not of himself righteous, because there is no one who is righteous. (See Romans 3:10.) It is the righteousness of God through Christ that is operating in his or her life. Through wisdom, the righteous person lives righteously by following the example set by Christ. However, if a righteous man departs from righteousness, to practice and enjoy the pleasures of sin for a season, the righteous man will not be saved from destruction based on his past righteousness. (See Hebrews 11:28.)

In Ezekiel 33:12–13, the prophet explains how righteousness works and how deception regarding righteousness can be a death sentence, "Therefore, thou son of man, say unto the children of thy people, The righteousness of the righteous shall not deliver him in the day of his transgression (because transgression of the law is sin): as for the wickedness of the wicked, he shall not fall thereby in the day that he turneth from his wickedness; neither shall the righteous be able to live for his righteousness in the day that he sinneth. When I shall say to the righteous, that he shall surely live; if he trusts in his own righteousness, and commits iniquity, all his righteousnesses shall not be remembered; but for his iniquity that he hath committed, he shall die." Ezekiel is issuing a warning. A wise man will hear it and live. This warning is the voice of wisdom.

WISDOM'S VOICE

> Wisdom crieth without; she uttereth her voice in the streets:
> She crieth in the chief place of concourse, in the openings
> of the gates: in the city she uttereth her words, saying, How
> long, ye simple ones, will ye love simplicity? and the scorn-
> ers delight in their scorning, and fools hate knowledge?
> Turn you at my reproof: behold, I will pour out my spirit
> unto you, I will make known my words unto you.
>
> —PROVERBS 1:20–23

What I notice about wisdom is that it speaks wherever people gather, work, play, meet, shop, use public transit, and live. Wisdom speaks to help us avoid deception. Every place that people go in the world, the voice of wisdom is there speaking to the people. When we go outside, or if we are on our way to work, wisdom is there calling. In the marketplace, on the highways and busy streets, in the city, and in the country wisdom is calling. In homes, in government, at the gym, or at a picnic, in churches, wisdom is speaking and calling to us. To the rich, to the poor, to kings and queens, to governors and heads of state, to moms and dads, to the old and young alike, wisdom is calling. Wisdom will never stop speaking. Time after time Jesus calls. When wisdom renders a rebuke, turn away from sin. Do not harden your heart as they did in the wilderness and provoked God. The Lord disciplines those whom He loves. As you pray and worship, God will release wisdom and strength.

Wisdom is calling to the wise in all nations and on every college campus. This is that high calling of God that must be positively answered. This high calling is the ministry of reconciliation. God reconciled us to Himself through Jesus Christ and gave us a min-istry of reconciliation. Now, this wisdom is at work in us to recon-cile the whole world to God. This ministry will open the eyes of the blind and turn them from darkness to light, help them receive forgiveness of sins, and an inheritance among the sanctified. (See Acts 20:23.) If we who are called do not pay attention to and obey wisdom's instructions, we will be the blind leading the blind, and both the blind and the leader will fall into a ditch.

CHAPTER 19

God Has Sent Watchmen Into the World

I
N EVERY GENERATION there are ambassadors, intercessors, prophets, and messengers who speak to the nations through wisdom regarding the perfect will of God for mankind and the plan of Satan to destroy mankind. God will do absolutely nothing without first speaking to these messengers. Whether the people receive this wisdom with joy and gladness or not, the messenger must speak. If the prophet speaks as God has commanded, giving directions and instructions, then the responsibility for what happens to the people rests with the people. If they listen to the watchman and follow instructions, they will be saved. Again, whether the people respond appropriately or not, the watchman must speak the word of the Lord. The will of God is for the people to obey. If the watchman does not speak, the blood of the people will be upon his head. Here is what the prophet Ezekiel says about the ministry of the watchman:

> Again the word of the LORD came unto me, saying, Son of man, speak to the children of thy people, and say unto them, When I bring the sword upon a land, if the people of the land take a man of their coasts, and set him for their watchman: If when he seeth the sword come upon the land,

he blow the trumpet, and warn the people; then whosoever heareth the sound of the trumpet, and taketh not warning; if the sword come, and take him away, his blood shall be upon his own head. He heard the sound of the trumpet, and took not warning; his blood shall be upon him. But he that taketh warning shall deliver his soul. But if the watchman see the sword come, and blow not the trumpet, and the people be not warned; if the sword come, and take any person from among them, he is taken away in his iniquity; but his blood will I require at the watchman's hand.

—Ezekiel 33:1–6

Armies of watchmen are being chosen by God from among the nations to be trained in spiritual warfare for the Last Days. These watchmen will be heads of state, ambassadors, diplomats, confidants, bishops, missionaries, strategic military planners, and armed forces. I believe that Pope John Paul II was a watchman. I pray that his mantle has fallen on Pope Benedict XVI. The secular world and the body of believers need wise-hearted, knowledge-able watchmen who possess understanding in all aspects of life. Every nation needs watchmen. When President George W. Bush established the Department of Homeland Security, I believe that it was a part of God's plan for the end times. The head of this department will be a watchman. Our government followed a spiritual and Biblical example in establishing this department. The original goal of the watchman was to sound the alarm, warning the people of impending danger.

The watchmen of the Last Days will be men and women from all walks of life, and from every nation, tongue, and tribe on the face of the earth. Even now, the agents of this special force of watchmen are being placed in strategic positions by the Lord. Their mission will be more involved than the watchmen described in Ezekiel 33. They will be experts in spiritual warfare, operating under a new and better covenant than Ezekiel had. They will possess wisdom, knowledge, and understanding; the authority of the Name; the power of the Blood; and the longevity of the Word. They will know how to overcome the accuser of the brethren by the blood of the Lamb, the word of their testimony, and by not loving their lives unto death. (See Revelation 12:10–11.) They will be prayer experts who hold back the antichrist and his kingdom until the Gospel has been preached to every nation and the fullness of the Gentiles is in effect. These agents will know how to activate the following weapons of war:

1. "The blast of the breath of the nostrils of God" (Ps. 18:15).

2. "The consuming fire and devouring flame of God" (Deut. 9:3; Isa. 29:6).

3. "The Word which is like a hammer crushing the residue of the enemy's work" (Jer. 23:29).

4. The "new threshing instrument having teeth" (Isa. 41:15).

EZEKIEL'S VISION

Out of the army of watchmen, a power force will arise. God gave Ezekiel a vision of four spirit beings and their assigned work in the heavens. With precision and skill these four work before the Lord of heaven and earth. I believe that God revealed to Ezekiel a heavenly pattern in the spiritual realm of something that would become a reality on the earth. Here is an excerpt from Ezekiel's vision, "Also out of the midst thereof came the likeness of four living creatures. And this was their appearance; they had the likeness of a man. And every one had four faces, and every one had four wings. And their feet were straight feet; and the sole of their feet was like the sole of a calf's foot: and they sparkled like the colour of burnished brass. And they had the hands of a man under their wings on their four sides. Their wings were joined one to another; they turned not when they went; they went every one straight forward. As for the likeness of their faces, they four had the face of a man, and the face of a lion, on the right side: and they four had the face of an ox on the left side; they four also had the face of an eagle. Thus were their faces: and their wings were stretched upward; two wings of every one were joined one to another, and two covered their bodies. And they went every one straight forward: whither the spirit was to go, they went; and they turned not when they went." (See Ezekiel 1:5–12.)

Through Ezekiel's revelation we get a vision of supernatural ability that will be given to human beings. This small special force of four beings conduct spiritual warfare in heaven. Their movement was one single movement, not four separate activities. Not one of them broke rank. Not one of them was out of step. Not one moved in the opposite direction of the Spirit of God. They moved with 100 percent accuracy under the leadership of a certain man. They were completely focused on the Spirit of God within the man. These beings moved and worked together in perfect harmony with precision and skill. The leader of this four-man force was so honored, respected and revered, that the force had the appearance of their leader. It was under the man's leadership that they understood their call to excellence. They were chosen not because they were great, but because they had great respect and honor for their leadership and understood the power of unity. Because the Spirit of excellence was upon their lives, they operated in unity. They were unified with their leader and also with one another.

In my opinion, the four-man force under the leadership of this man is a shadow of the small armies that will destroy multitudes of enemy forces in the battle of Armageddon. Ezekiel identifies them as cherubim. I call them the wisdom force.

CHAPTER 20

The Wisdom Force

WHEN GOD GAVE Ezekiel this vision, He allowed him to see tremendous detail about these four spirit beings. The vision and the symbolism in the vision are not without purpose. This historical record is not just an unusual vision given to the prophet Ezekiel. I believe that God wants each generation to discover why He had Ezekiel write this vision, and what the vision means, based on the information that He revealed. The wisdom force is based on what I believe God has revealed to me regarding Ezekiel's vision.

God will activate the wisdom force according to the appointed time for the purpose of the gathering in of the final harvest of souls. He is the Lord of Hosts, Commander In Chief of the wisdom force. The wisdom force is a force of four special agents, one man from the north, one from the south, one from the east, and one from the west representing all nations. There will be many four man wisdom force agents in all nations under God's command. Some will be family men having one wife. They will be faithful and gentle husbands and fathers who operate in the office of bishop. (See 1 Timothy 3:1–7.) Some will be single men. All wisdom force agents will serve the true and living God, the only wise God. Compassion and mercy is their trademark. Their mission:

120

1. To invade the enemy's camp and destroy the plan of the one who plots day and night to kill, steal, and destroy the people of the Most High God.

2. To support believers.

3. To rescue those who have been called to become heirs of salvation.

4. To literally "raze hell."

5. They will be instrumental in helping believers "withhold the "mystery of iniquity" until the time of the fullness of the Gentiles. (See 2 Thessalonians 2:6–7.)

The force employs three techniques that make them indestructible. They work so closely with the Holy Spirit that their maneuvers can never be discovered by enemy experts. Their wisdom strategy is profound, yet simple. It consists of these three major components: 1.) communion with the Lord, 2.) unity with their leadership and each other, and 3.) instant obedience. This puts the force on the cutting edge and gives them power over all the power of the enemy. The chosen will be given supernatural ability and miraculous power. They will be filled with the Spirit of God in wisdom, knowledge, and understanding. They will have keen insight, creative thoughts and ideas, and will be skilled in all manner of learning every kind of futuristic strategy, technique, and concept. Assisting the wisdom force will be the "four spirits of the heavens, which go forth from standing before the Lord of all the earth" (Zech. 6:5). The wisdom force will have a spiritual force of angelic beings who will work very closely with them to defeat principalities, powers, rulers of the darkness of this world, and wickedness in high places. (See Ephesians 6:12.) Worship and prayer will activate the spiritual force, putting them into action immediately.

The wisdom force will master unprecedented maneuvers and complete great exploits that have not been attempted in the history of mankind. They will understand and honor the position of leadership. They will also understand the power of unity. Because they know and have the heart of their leader, God will give spiritual instructions to these spiritual men who will move without fail by the Spirit, in the spirit, and with the Spirit of God. For this reason, this force will never be led astray by the deception of the enemy—never.

This force will possess vast knowledge of covert operations, and the secrets and mysteries of God will be revealed to them. A flash of lightening is the unit of measure used to determine the amount of time it takes for them to receive knowledge and enlightenment. From a central location agents will be instructed, briefed, and strategically sent into diverse regions of the world. On certain occasions, they will be translated by the Spirit of God from nation to nation. God alone will decide which nations need their expertise for survival. They will complete the work of God in remote places of the earth, preparing the way for the coming of the King of Kings and Lord of Lords. Before the Second Coming of the Lord with thousands of His angels, the wisdom force will have made the way sure for the Gospel to be preached to the nations of people in the 10/40 Window. The prayers of the faithful are critical. The Lord will find faith on the earth when He comes.

Sensitive, alert, and attentive to the Spirit of God, the force will not be motivated by selfish instincts. Their energy and power will come from the Holy Spirit. They know this quite well and will acknowledge that God is the center of their joy and the source of their strength. Their operations will always be precise and quick. The precision, skill, and expertise which they employ is determined by the fashion of their design. Their design is the same as that of the four spirit beings, however it is invisible.

It can be seen and discerned "in the spirit." It is their design (four individual beings, each with four different faces, with their wings all existing in the likeness of one man) that will cause them to do the impossible. Their design contains all of the ingredients for success, and none can stop or defeat them. Their weapons of war are not like any known to man. These weapons are spiritual and will be used to pull down all manner of evil and wicked strongholds. Through their operations, all of the kingdoms of the god of this world will crumble. The worldwide black market will come to a halt and collapse.

Wisdom force agents will defeat enemy forces supernaturally. They will not be seen or detected, except by the gift of discerning of spirits because they will move only by the Spirit. They will go unnoticed. Only the results of their work will be seen (gathering of the heirs of salvation). A flash of lightning will be the evidence of their movement, indicating "mission complete."

Knowledge about the force will not deter its effectiveness. No military experts anywhere in the world will be able to duplicate or destroy the wisdom force. The wisdom force can never be captured because of their ability to be translated by God from one place to another. Governments will pay scientists from around the world billions of dollars to study the wisdom force to find the source of their power. It will be a costly, but futile, effort.

The wisdom force emblem will depict the four faces captured in the heart of the man. The emblem will be symbolic of four majestic aspects of the character and nature of God multiplied in the life of each agent. The four faces indicate that each agent has equally profound leadership qualities in four distinct areas.

The face of the man represents the human character, a living soul created in the image and likeness of God with faith, wisdom, understanding, knowledge, skill, ability, intelligence, power, and the distinct ability to choose between good and evil. All of these characteristics are seen in the first man, Adam. However, this "soul nature" caused the first man Adam to disobey God. As a result of Adam's disobedience, all mankind would die. However, through the last Adam, Jesus Christ, all mankind can be quickened or made alive and given the gift of eternal life. "For since by man [Adam] came death, by [one] man [Jesus Christ] came also the resurrection of the dead" (1 Cor. 15:21). The face of the man does not represent the Adamic nature which is dominated by the soul, but the recreated spiritual man. This man is born again by the Spirit of God with ability to speak things that do not exist into existence.

The face of the lion represents strength, power, and fearlessness. Authority and power over all the power of the enemy has been awarded to the wisdom force. They know how to exert that power to get desired results. Boldfaced, their faces set like a flint, they have a "won't back down for any reason" attitude. They move straight ahead not looking to the left or the right. Hindering forces cannot obstruct God's plan. Fiery darts aimed at the wisdom force will return to their source. No barriers can stop the action of the wisdom force. Neither can any weapon of war defeat the force: concrete walls, underground bunkers, steel reinforcements, nuclear, biological, chemical, or technological warfare. Technologies of warfare not yet discovered by man will be unable to stand against or defeat the wisdom force. No weapon, past, present, or future formed against the wisdom force will prosper. The evidence of their courage and bravery is seen in the face of the lion.

The face of the ox represents humility and compassion. Humility will bring the necessary balance into the character of the wisdom force. No military force can complete its work with perfection without humbling itself under the mighty hand of God. Compassion for the innocent, the poor, lost, destitute, discouraged, and dying is the greatest asset the wisdom force possesses. These two perfectly balanced character traits open the door to unimaginable opportunities for the wisdom force. God exceeds their heart's desire, blessing them exceeding abundantly above all that they can ask or think.

The face of the eagle represents the ability to soar to supernatural heights beyond the galaxies and into heaven. There they bow before the throne of the great Jehovah. From this vantage point, they clearly see the whole picture and know the truth in every situation as they engage in strategic planning with the Lord. This face also represents clarity of thought, insight, a sharp mind, creativity, and the absolute absence of confusion. This force can meet in heaven, on the earth, underneath the earth, or in the ocean. They can manifest in the flesh or they can operate in the invisible. They are just as effective in either form. The face of the eagle also represents freedom and liberty to move without restraint.

The four-man wisdom force will have one Leader, the Lord Jesus Christ. They will be so unified with Him that they will look exactly like Him. It is through Him they take form and exist. He is their only source of strength and power. He is the One who leads the force through heaven and earth to complete great exploits. It is through this Man, the Lord Jesus Christ, that the force will live and move. The wisdom force is nothing without Him. He is their source of health and enlightenment. He is their life. Just as the "mystery of iniquity" is already working evil, the wisdom force is at work spreading the goodness of God among men and women everywhere.

In a time of great distress and unprecedented tribulations, the wisdom force will rescue the innocent from the hand of the enemy. "For then shall be great tribulation, such as was not since the beginning of the world to this time, no, nor ever shall be. And except those days should be shortened, there should no flesh be saved: but for the elect's sake those days shall be shortened. Then if any man shall say unto you, Lo, here is Christ, or there; believe it not" (Matt. 24:21–23). During this time, false prophets, false Christs, and imposters will show signs and wonders and deceive many. The wisdom force will be on assignment to bind these strongmen and destroy their lying signs and wonders. The imposters will be very convincing. They will look and act like Christ and His representatives. If it were possible, even the very elect of God would be deceived and led astray by these imposters, but the wisdom and enlightenment of God that emanates from the wisdom force will assist the elect and keep them from falling into deception, depression, and degradation.

CHRIST IS AT WORK THROUGH THE WISDOM FORCE

The symbolism in Ezekiel's vision of the four spirits with their four faces gives us insight into God's true love for the world. The "Captain of Salvation" was perfected through the things that He suffered, and through God's grace, He died for every man. (See Hebrews 2:9–10.) Represented in the vision is the life and ministry of Jesus Christ. He is referred to as the Lion of the tribe of Judah. He has been given the gift of divine power, possessing power to lay His life down and the power to take it up again. The ox represents the sacrificial lamb offered for the sins of the world. "I was like a lamb or an ox that is brought to the slaughter; and I knew not that they had devised devices against Me" (Jer. 11:19). The eagle symbolizes unrestrained freedom. Christ is the Lord from heaven. "Now the Lord is that Spirit: and where the Spirit of the Lord is, there is liberty" (2 Cor. 3:17). The man represents Jesus, the Christ, born of a woman, God incarnate. He is the great High Priest who can "be touched with the feeling of our infirmities"; He "was in all points tempted like as we are, yet without sin" (Heb. 4:15). All of these portraits of the Lord's character come together in the likeness of a Man, the invisible God who is seen in the face of Jesus Christ.

FOUR CULTURES REPRESENTING THE NATIONS OF THE EARTH

The four faces represent four diverse cultures that are scattered throughout the earth. These four diverse cultures represent great multitudes of people from the north, south, east, and west which no man can number of all nations, people, tongues, and tribes who will stand before the throne of God. They are the sanctified who have been washed in the blood of the Lamb.

The eagle represents nations of believers of the Christian faith from around the world. By far, Christians are the largest religious group in the world today. The majority of Christians are located in the United States. The symbol of the United States is the American eagle. The bald eagle represents the Spirit of God in freedom and liberty, and the pursuit of excellence.

The lion represents the people of the Hindu faith from around the world. The majority of the people of India are Hindu. The national emblem of India is four lions standing together. The fourth lion, which is in back, cannot be seen. In Ezekiel's vision, each of the four spirits had one face, which was that of a lion. This four-lion emblem of India may have been developed from Ezekiel's vision. The lion symbolizes power and strength.

The ox, often known as the beast of burden, is representative of the animal used in worship under the old covenant by the Hebrew nation. A Jewish priest would once a year make the atonement for the sins of the people through animal sacrifice made under very specific conditions. The term *ox* is used at least 145 times in Scripture and is generally associated with sacrificial offering. Judaism represents a great number of the faithful worldwide. The majority of its followers reside in Israel.

The face of the man could represent Buddha, as well as other religions that worship deified gods. Buddhism is the major religion of China. The Buddha, a prince, spent his life searching for spiritual enlightenment, insight, and wisdom. The symbol for Buddhism is a man seated in a yoga position for meditation. Some of the Buddha statues are seated with the legs straight.

When the Lord Jesus Christ returns, all of the religious walls that separate cultures, nations, and people will be broken down. The nations will be united under one Man. The wisdom force will be instrumental in turning people from sin unto God. The power of Christ through the Gospel will persuade multitudes upon multitudes to come out of the valley of decision and make a positive and definite decision for Christ. As they cry salvation to our God who sits upon the throne and unto the Lamb, the power of God will usher the world into a new spiritual dimension. Then, the kingdom of God will greatly increase, and the kingdom of darkness will greatly diminish.

CHAPTER 21

In the Darkest Hour, Wisdom Will Speak

O NE OF THE darkest moments of my life came at a time when I was working inside the kingdom. All hell had broken loose! I was devastated and deeply hurt. As the pain grew worse, I became very angry. My anger turned into bitterness, and bitterness was destroying me. At the same time, I was reaping an overflow of the blessings of God in my life. I had been listed in *Who's Who Among America's Teachers*. My income had dramatically increased within a twenty-four hour period and I sowed a substantial offering into good soil. I had been healed of a serious debilitating back injury. I did not understand what was happening, because both light and darkness, good and evil, life and death were present with me. Then, the voice of wisdom began to speak to me and this is what I perceived from the Spirit of God, *Prosperity and persecutions go hand in hand. When prosperity comes so do persecutions. Change is coming and you can either flow with the wind of change or be swept away by it.* Well, I knew that if I wanted to live and not die, I had to accept change. So I decided that I was going to move with the wind of change, *The purpose of the prosperity is to usher you into a new life with grace and ease.*

At this time there was no doubt that God's favor was working in my life in such an unprecedented way. I could not deny His presence and power. I stopped fighting my own battle and released circumstances, individuals, and those things that pertained to life and godliness to God. I could not allow my present circumstances to separate me from God's sweet love. His love surrounding me was the only treasure that kept me together. I surrendered all to Him, packed my bags and left, closing the door on that chapter of my life forever. When I left, through God's miraculous power, I was clothed and in my right mind. The change was like a breath of fresh air in paradise.

PARADISE

To me, exercising wisdom is like being in paradise. In His darkest hour, Jesus, the Wisdom of God, said these words to one of the thieves who was beside Him on the cross: "Today, [you will] be with me in paradise" (Luke 23:43). This is a demonstration of the wisdom of God in action. These were not just idle words. They were words of resurrection life and power. They were the wisest words ever spoken to a person on death row, and they were the most compassionate. No greater words will ever be spoken to someone who is about to be put to death for a crime that he has committed. Christ alone can remove the sting of death with the promise of paradise.

The Lord was speaking to the one thief who had asked to be remembered, but He chose the words that He spoke for the other thief who was listening. In other words, Wisdom spoke to one criminal, and for the other criminal. He knew that the reluctant thief was paying attention to the conversation between Himself and the wise thief. So, He carefully chose the word *paradise* to entice the reluctant one to long for a better life than the one he had lived thus far. Jesus also knew that the word *paradise* had a deep connotation. The Greek word for paradise is *paradesos*, and it means an Eden or a place of future happiness.

When I hear the word *paradise*, I immediately think of plush, deep, green forests with breathtaking wooded areas in a temperature of about eighty-five degrees with a brook flowing down a steep rocky slope, waterfalls, and an array of colorful wildflowers growing nearby. On the ocean side, there are sandy beaches with a warm ocean breeze and clear ocean water. The aroma of tropical fruit fills the streets and marketplaces. In open markets, beautiful indigenous people sell their artifacts before they reach the European and U.S. markets. It is a place of relaxation and basking in the beauty of His holiness. Anybody in his or her right mind would want to go to paradise.

Jesus chose the word *paradise* to instill a desire for something good, a desire for the supernatural. He wanted to instill a hunger and thirst for righteousness, a longing to know the invisible God who created paradise, and a vision of heaven in the mind of a hardened criminal. Jesus was expressing His love for a dying soul. He did not care that this man had mocked ·Him. I can imagine Jesus quoting Elizabeth Browning to this man, "How do I love thee? Let me count the ways." Jesus stood between life and death for him. For a moment, He held death captive allowing the opportunity for the enslaved to be set free and choose life.

THE STONY HEART

The Lord gave me insight into the reluctant thief. He was not insane, but he did have issues. The issues of life, and the cares of the world had hardened his heart. He was void of wisdom and understanding. Then, the god of this world blinded his mind because he was an unbeliever. So, he could not see the light of the glorious Gospel. Even when the Lord Jesus Christ was right beside him on the cross, this sinner could not see God. Only the pure in heart can see God. A hard heart will never see God. This man had allowed sin to take control of his life, therefore he could not receive the free gift of eternal life. He was a slave to sin, because whoever commits sin is sin's slave, and is owned by an invisible force. He no longer belonged to himself. He belonged to Satan the invisible slave owner. This is the reason why he could not visualize the beauty of paradise or receive everlasting life. So he refused the paradise offer. He was not a free man any more. When sin finished with him, it brought forth his death.

The statement, "Today, you will be with Me in paradise," is a synopsis of the greatest love story ever written. This statement is so rich and appealing. It is powerful and dramatic. It illustrates the power of God's unending love operating in its fullest measure at the transition point of death. The dramatic is illustrated as the bridegroom prepares to take the bride to paradise.

When this statement was uttered, time stood still, death was silenced, and put on hold. It was paralyzed and could not speak. Death had to obey God and stand still (as one who could not walk), and stand mute (as one who is deaf and dumb), until the man made his choice. The wisdom of God was wooing a soul to make a choice to let go and forget the ugly past of the thief and murderer, and receive life and become a new creation in Christ. This was not a new strategy. This is exactly what happened to Moses, David, Paul, and others whose life stories are recorded in the Old and New Testaments. God wanted to take a broken life and transform it. The results of the transformation could have been a great deliverer like Moses, a great king like David, or an extraordinary writer like Paul. In all eternity with God, there remains the opportunity for the lost to choose between eternal life and death. This is the wisdom of God.

Epilogue

How will you know when wisdom is working in your life? You will tell parables as Jesus did. You will win three thousand souls to Christ in one day as Peter did. You will have childlike faith as the Syrophoenician did. As a shepherd you will lead people out of bondage and into freedom as Moses did. Like Abraham you will become a father of many nations. You will write epistles as Paul did. You will sing psalms of praise and worship like David. You will be a compassionate kinsman-redeemer like Boaz. You will intercede like Israel did. You will prophesy like Isaiah. You will go on missionary journeys and evangelize the world as the disciples did. You will weep over your city as Jeremiah did for Jerusalem. You will rule over all the land like Joseph. You will interpret dreams like Daniel. You will be translated by the Spirit from one place to another like Philip. You will be ever-interceding as the Holy Spirit. You will use common sense. You will speak Proverbs as Solomon did.